KNEBWORTH
THROUGH TIME
Hugh Madgin

AMBERLEY PUBLISHING

Acknowledgements

This book would not have appeared without considerable support from a number of people: the generous assistance of Peter Allam, Mrs Patricia Aspinall, Entech, Clare Fleck, Archivist Knebworth House, Derek Fleming, Mrs & Mrs K. Follett, Doreen Hamid, Mr V. Harris, Danny King, Nathan Kitto, Knebworth Golf Club, John Law, the Moules family, Brian Norman, David Percival, Ken Stevens, David Stewart, Ruth Stratton, Curator, Stevenage Museum, Tony Tomlinson, Trussells Butchers and Julia and Tim Wise in providing photographs and information that has proved crucial. To them I would like to record my grateful thanks. Special thanks are also due to my wife Cath for her unfailing support.

First published 2011

Amberley Publishing
The Hill, Stroud
Gloucestershire, GL5 4EP

www.amberley-books.com

Copyright © Hugh Madgin, 2011

The right of Hugh Madgin to be identified as the Author of this work has been asserted in accordance with the Copyrights, Designs and Patents Act 1988.

ISBN 978 1 84868 092 0

British Library Cataloguing in Publication Data.
A catalogue record for this book is available from the British Library.

Typeset in 9.5pt on 12pt Celeste.
Typesetting by Amberley Publishing.
Printed in the UK.

Introduction

Thanks to its enormously successful music festivals, held since the 1970s, the name Knebworth is recognised worldwide. Owing to the presence of Knebworth House, home of the Lytton family since 1490, Knebworth and its people have featured prominently in national life over the centuries. A village still, with a population of just fewer than 5,000, Knebworth is a post town and in these pages the associated villages of Datchworth and Woolmer Green are also featured as they are included in the Knebworth (SG3) area.

Knebworth began as a small settlement midway between the Old London Road to the west and what would later become the Great North Road to the east. The site of the original village is today the location of St Mary's church and Knebworth House, in the park laid out by Sir William Lytton in the seventeenth century. Described as a 'denuded' rather than deserted medieval village, this settlement was replaced by one between the old medieval Great Park of Knebworth and Sir William's park, the latter of which today is a substantial tourist attraction.

In 1884, the opening of a station on the Great Northern Railway main line between Deards End and the Great North Road led to the creation of a new village, which would be called first 'Knebworth Station' and later 'New Knebworth'. Eventually, in 1925, the village alongside Knebworth Park was given the name Old Knebworth and the new settlement became simply Knebworth.

With the exception of Old Cottage and Plum Cottage – both of which are in Gun Lane – along with buildings at Deards End, no building in 'New Knebworth' dates back to before the 1880s.

Datchworth, like the original settlement of Knebworth, is a hilltop village established before the Domesday survey, while Woolmer Green grew up on the Great North Road after that road was improved in the eighteenth century, presaging the similar development of 'New Knebworth' a mile to the north a hundred years later. Bulls Green is at the south of the parish of Datchworth.

Plans were drawn up before the First World War by the Knebworth Estate for an 800-acre Garden Village to be built around the Great North Road, with a street plan devised by the architect Sir Edwin Lutyens. In the event, the development of a second 'Garden City' near Welwyn and the start of the era of council house building that followed the First World War meant that the Garden Village never came to fruition, but a factory was constructed at Woolmer Green and houses, built and managed by a co-operative housing trust at Stockens Green, were erected.

Much of 'New Knebworth' was, in fact, part of the parish of Datchworth until a rearrangement of boundaries in 1911; indeed, the cast-iron milepost at the corner of London Road and Station Road, marking the 28 miles' distance from London, still bears the words 'Datchworth Parish'.

Today Knebworth is a busy commuter village and further expansion within its Green Belt location is unlikely; there is just one field between it and Woolmer Green on its south side and the same between the village and the Hertford Loop railway line, which forms the boundary with Stevenage New Town on the east. Away from the bustle of the commuter village along London Road, the parish retains some very out-of-the-way corners such as Pigeonswick, Rustling End and Rye End.

Thanks to its close association with Lutyens, who married into the Lytton family, Knebworth is well provided with buildings of architectural interest. However, its most remarkable building has to be Knebworth House, remodelled between 1811 and 1883 to the designs of John Biagio Rebecca and H. E. Kendall. Just as its grounds have achieved fame as the location for music festivals, so Knebworth House has become familiar to cinema-goers for being the location of many films.

Hugh Madgin
Stevenage, 2011

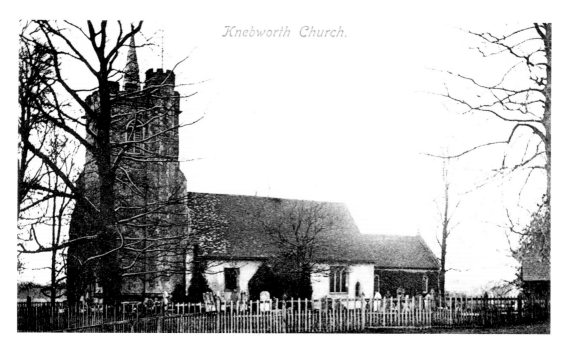

Knebworth Church.

St Mary's Church

The structure of the church of St Mary and St Thomas of Canterbury (normally referred to St Mary's) dates from the twelfth century. Its nave and chancel are thought to have been erected around 1120, but although the church was not specifically mentioned in the Domesday Book, its origins may well stretch back before the Norman Conquest.

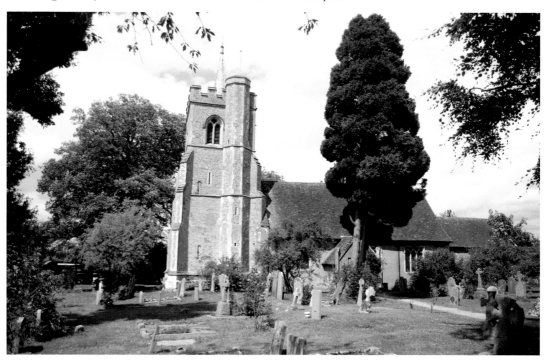

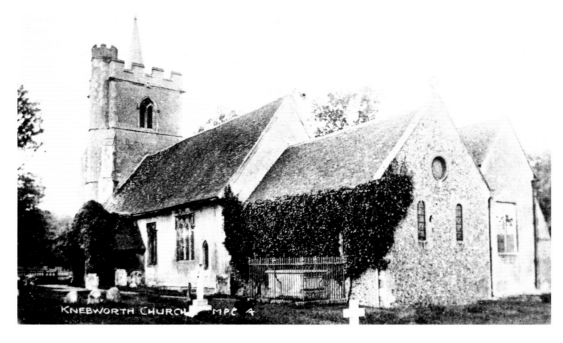

The Tomb of Leonora Robinson Lytton

The railed chest tomb alongside the chancel is that of Leonora Robinson Lytton, who died in 1790. She was the widow of John Robinson-Lytton and, after he died in 1762, she secretly married James Oswald, the Scottish composer and music publisher who had been appointed Chamber Composer to George III in 1761. Oswald became the master of Knebworth House until his death in 1769; the location of his grave is unknown.

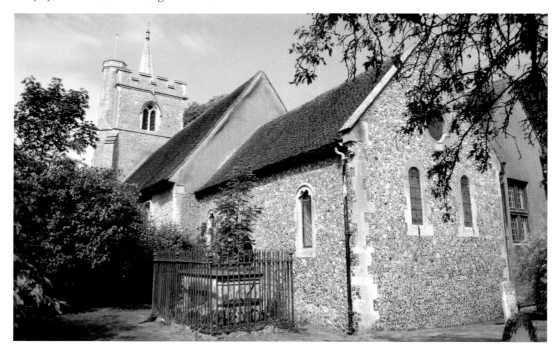

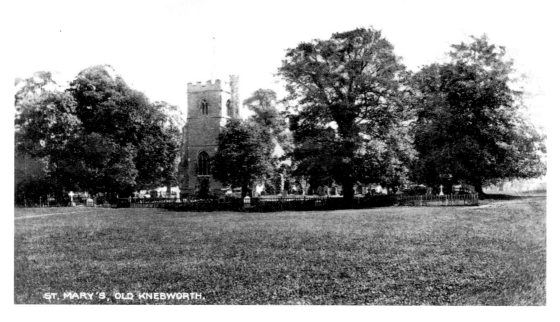

St. MARY'S, OLD KNEBWORTH.

St Mary's Church from the West
The tower of St Mary's was built by Sir John Hotoft in 1420. He was Lord of the Manor at the time and was Treasurer of the Household to Henry VI. His daughter, Agnes, married Sir Robert de Lytton of Derbyshire and in 1490 their grandson, Sir Robert Lytton, purchased the estate of Knebworth from his cousin's husband Sir Thomas Bourchie.

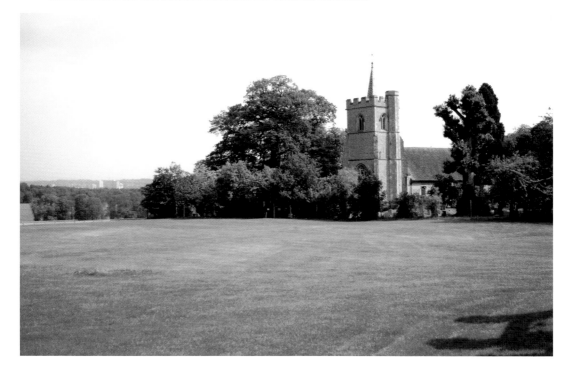

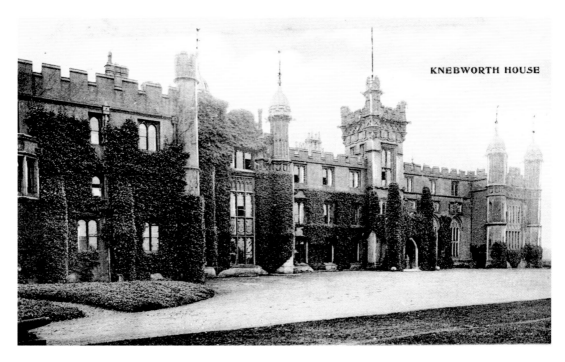

Knebworth House, East Front

The last rebuilding of Knebworth House took place in 1883 when a third storey was added to the Gothic building. The 'gothic fantasy' with its battlements, turrets, griffins and gargoyles, which has been so popular with film-makers over the years, has retained the same aspect since then. The building has a Grade II* listing.

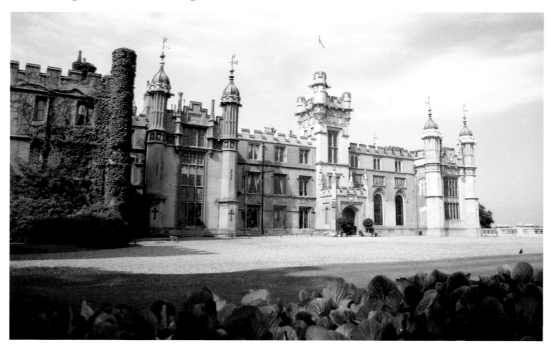

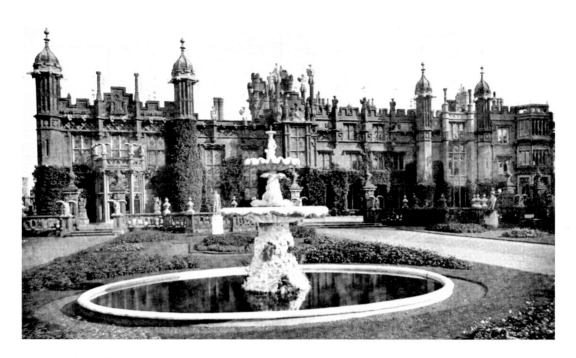

Knebworth House, West Front

The earlier view shows the gardens of Knebworth House as laid out to plans by Edward Bulwer Lytton, which were drawn up in 1845. In Victorian times the gardens required 36,000 annual bedding plants and the services of fourteen gardeners. The gardens were remodelled in the early twentieth century to the plans of Edwin Lutyens, the fountains and statues being superseded by lawns and avenues of pollarded lime trees.

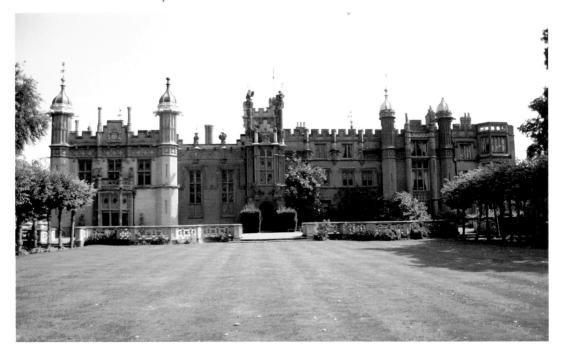

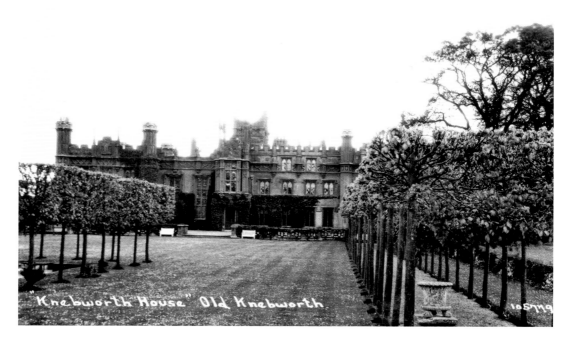

Knebworth House Formal Garden

Lutyens' Sunken Lawn and pollarded limes are seen shortly after the remodelling of the formal garden in the earlier view. It is hard to believe that beneath the sandstone cladding and decoration there are the remains of one wing of a sober brick mansion.

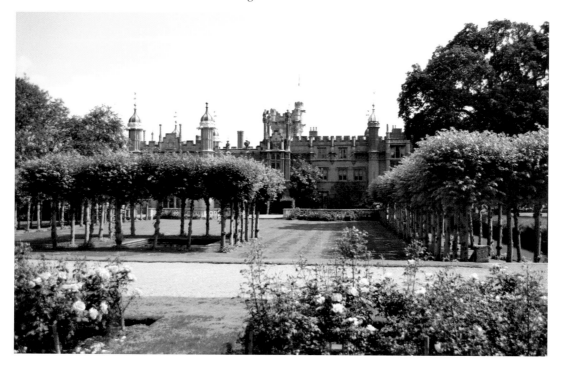

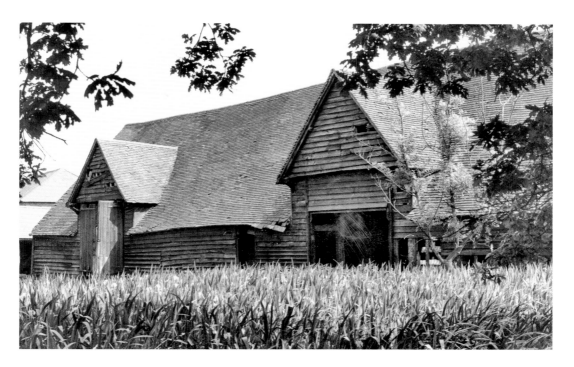

Lodge Farm Barn
Two barns were moved to Knebworth Park in 1971 and 1972 to form a catering complex. The first was from Manor Farm and was moved in one piece, while the other, pictured first in its original location, came from Lodge Farm. This structure is the newer of the two barns and dates from either the late seventeenth or early eighteenth century (David Percival).

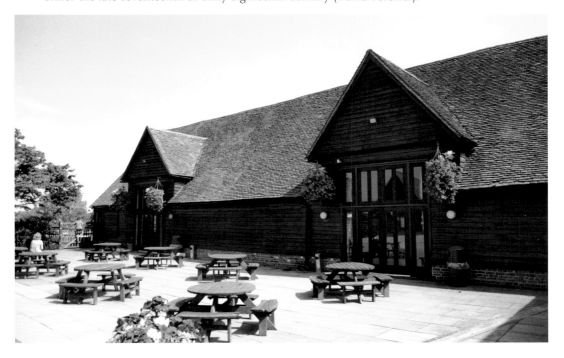

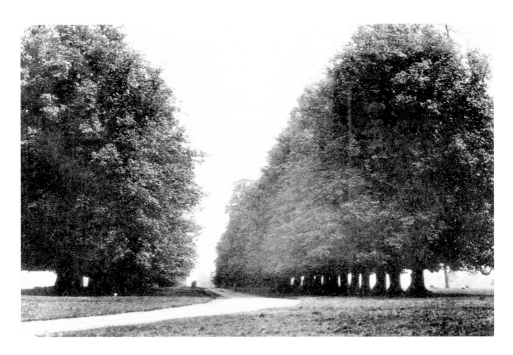

Knebworth Park Avenue
The top (south) end of the avenue, nearest the house. The concrete road laid around the park from Junction 7 of the A1(M) today follows the middle of the avenue, forming the start of the exit route for those leaving the park. This two-mile road, laid in 1971 at a cost of £50,000, has been crucial to the success of Knebworth Park as a tourist attraction.

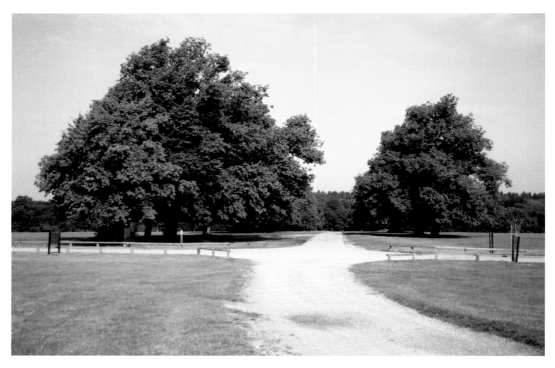

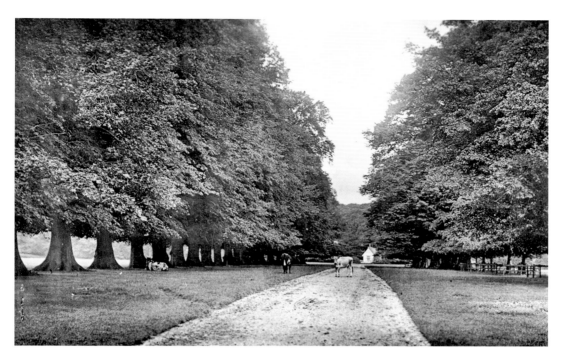

Avenue and Lake House

The avenue northwards from Knebworth House towards the lake is in fact one of four in the park. Today, tree growth around the lake has obscured the view of Lake House, even when the avenue is not busy with festival-goers, as seen here at the Sonisphere event of 2011.

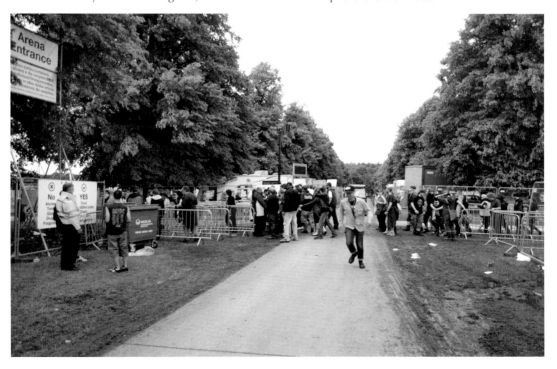

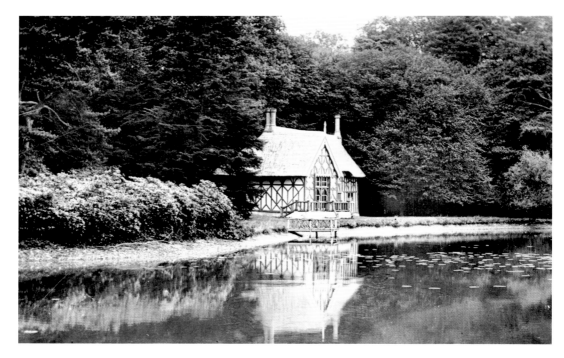

Knebworth Lake

Knebworth Lake was the largest expanse of water in the district before the creation of Fairlands Valley Park in nearby Stevenage. In the colder winters of the first half of the twentieth century, large crowds came here to skate on the ice.

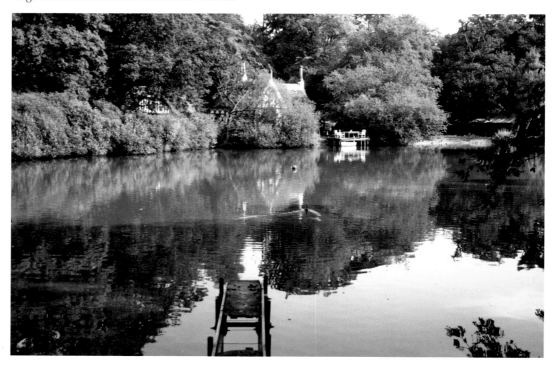

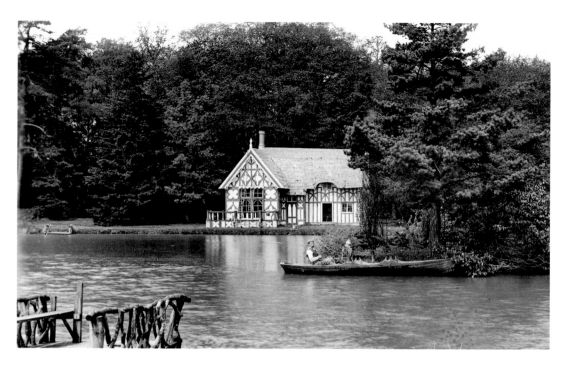

On Knebworth Lake

Although the lake in Knebworth has doubtless been enlarged as part of the landscaping of the park, there has always been a large expanse of water here, and it has even been suggested that this could have been the location of the mill at Knebworth mentioned in the Domesday survey. The register of listed buildings describes Lake House as a seventeenth-century building, remodelled during the nineteenth century (Knebworth House Archive).

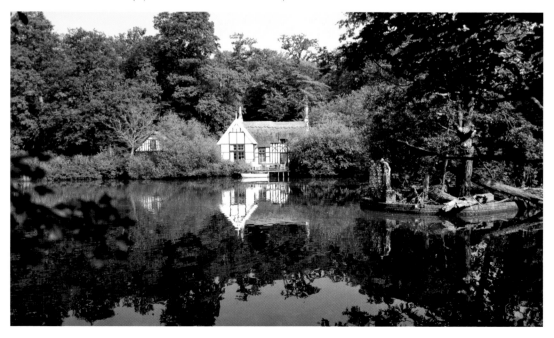

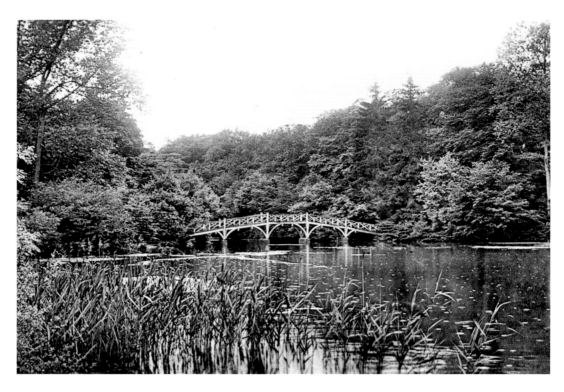

Knebworth Lake Bridge
The wooden bridge at the west end of Knebworth Lake has, in recent years, fallen into disrepair. In the earlier view it is seen from the east. The contemporary view shows its remains from the west.

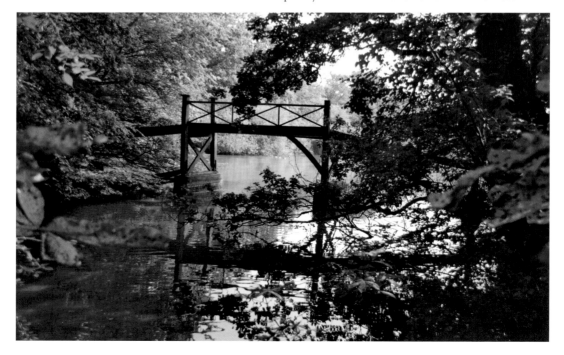

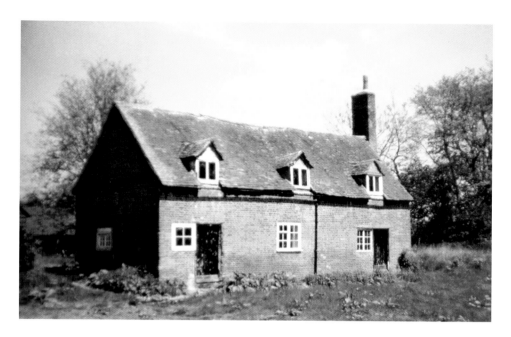

Keepers Cottage

This building, at one time two cottages, was in the park to the east of Knebworth Lake. Standing empty by the time of the earlier view, which was taken in 1971, it was demolished a year or two later. Its location can still be discerned by a flat spot on the gently sloping land and the bush that stood alongside its western boundary (Stevenage Museum).

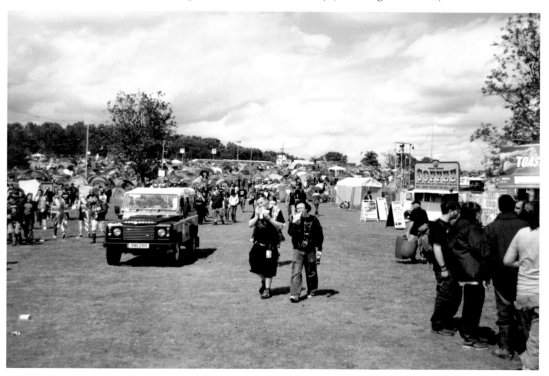

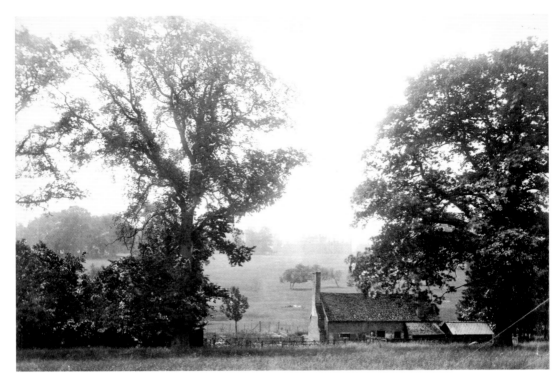

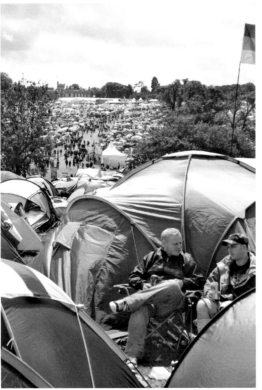

From Keepers Cottage

The imposing profile of Knebworth House is seen across the park from the rising ground behind Keepers Cottage in the earlier view. The contemporary view taken during the Sonisphere Festival in 2011 shows part of the campsite set up to accommodate the 60,000 attendees to the three-day rock festival (Knebworth House Archive).

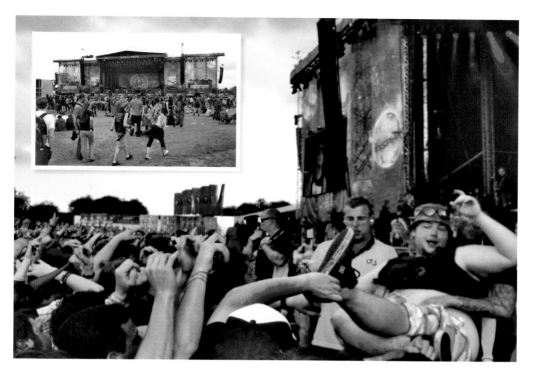

West Park

The largest of the five stages at the Sonisphere Festival of 2011 was the Apollo stage towards the west end of the park. Headlining acts of the festival such as Metallica, Megadeth, Slipknot and Limp Bizkit appeared here. Within days of the crowd-surfing exuberance at the front the vista from exactly the same spot had returned to sylvan parkland.

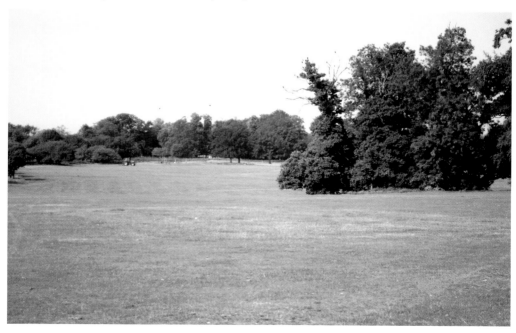

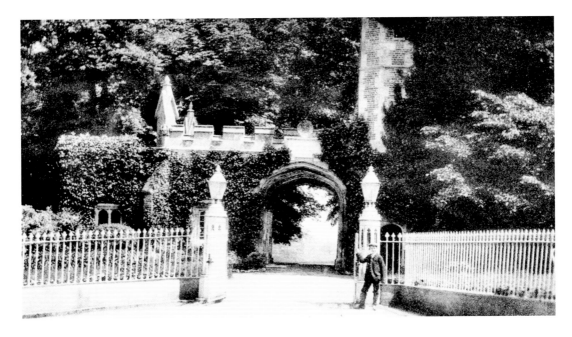

Tower Lodge

When Mrs Bulwer Lytton had the three wings of Knebworth House demolished in 1811, the materials from the old gatehouse that provided the entrance to the courtyard were taken to the south-west corner of the park, adjacent to the Old London Road, and reconstructed as Tower Lodge. After a period when its condition deteriorated, Tower Lodge was sold off by the Knebworth Estate.

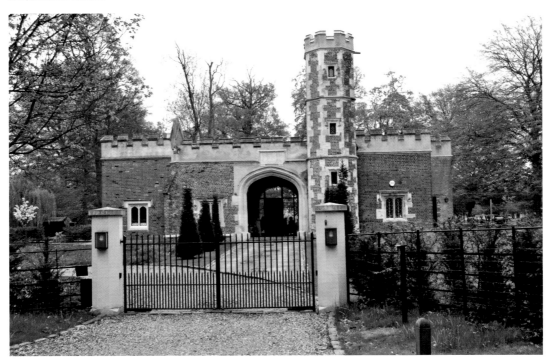

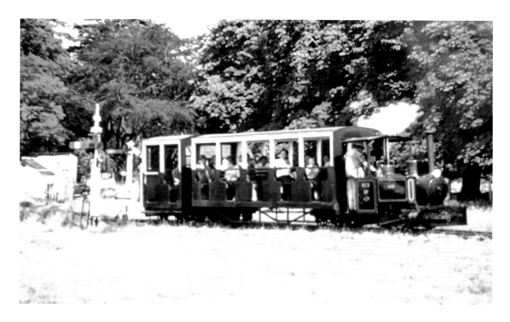

Knebworth West Park & Wintergreen Light Railway
Opening in 1971, the Knebworth West Park & Wintergreen Light Railway brought 2-ft gauge travel to Hertfordshire. Locomotives from other lines would visit on gala occasions. Here, *Rishra* from the Leighton Buzzard Railway gets away from Knebworth House station on 11 August 1984. The railway closed in 1990 and was replaced by Knebworth Miniature Railway. (Geoff Edwards)

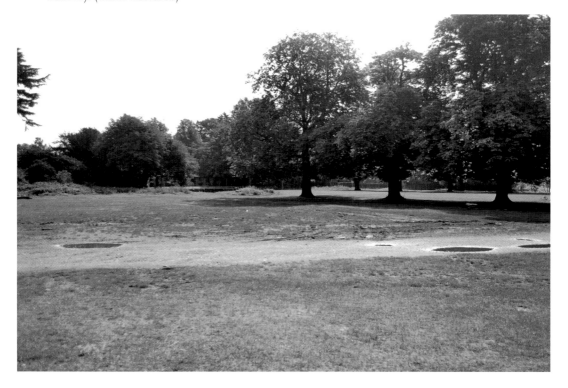

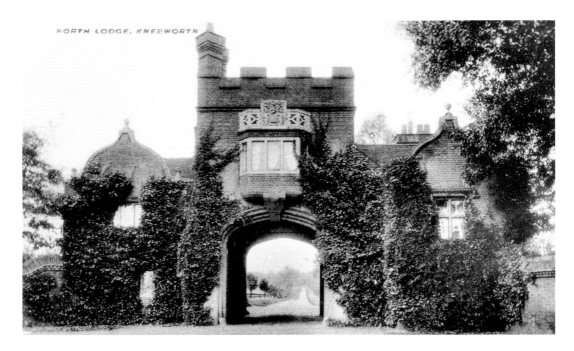

NORTH LODGE, KNEBWORTH

North Lodges

The North Lodges were built in 1883 on what was then known as Stevenage Road, later renamed Warren Spring Lane. This road was obliterated by the construction of the A1(M) Stevenage Bypass; the short section of it by the lodge, now used as the entrance to Knebworth Park, is all that remains. In the 1930s the manager of ICI's Game Research Estate lived here. This began in Knebworth Park in 1933, moved to Fordingbridge, Hampshire, in 1946 and is now the Game & Wildlife Conservation Trust.

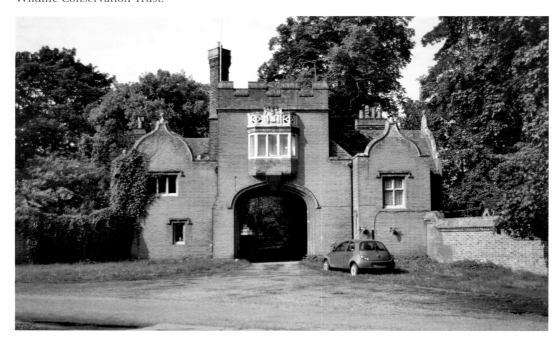

Old Knebworth Hill

The branch of the old Stevenage Road that led to Broadwater remains, although it has been diverted twice. The first time was at its eastern end when the construction of the Hertford Loop railway necessitated it being moved southwards to emerge on the Great North Road at the side of the Roebuck. Forty years later, a few hundred yards further west, a bridge was made for it to pass under the A1(M). Today the road is known as Old Knebworth Lane.

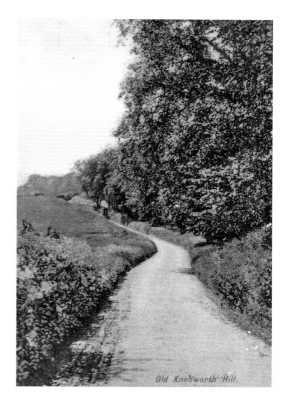

Old Knebworth Hill.

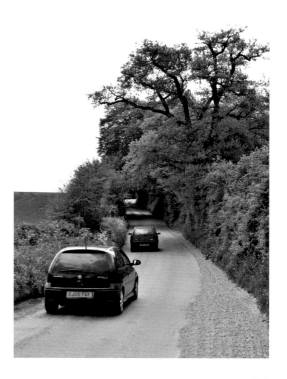

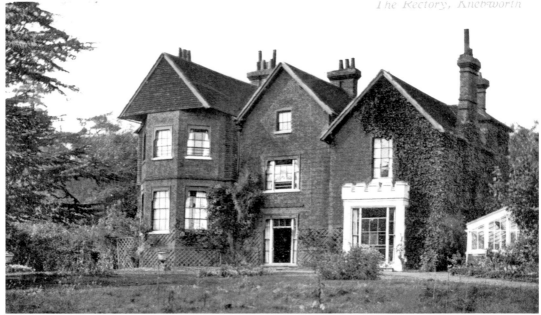

The Rectory

Now known as Glebe House, the former Knebworth Rectory is today the home of internationally successful novelist Ken Follett and his wife Barbara, who was Member of Parliament for the Stevenage constituency from 1997 to 2010. The Rectory was rebuilt in 1844 to the design of Henry Clutton; one of the barns on the site dates back to the seventeenth century.

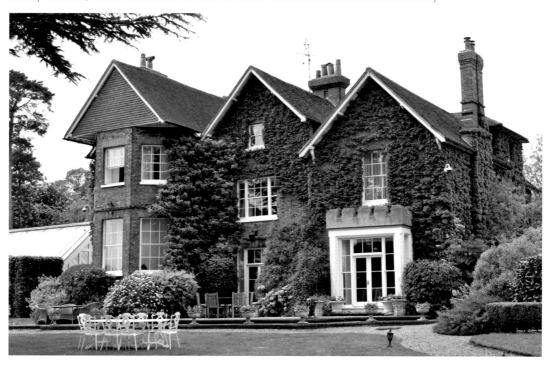

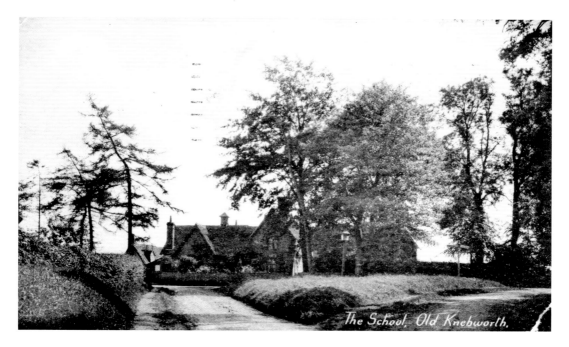

The School, Old Knebworth.

Old Knebworth: the School

This area was called Knebworth Green in the nineteenth century, a name which was echoed by a new development of fifteen houses along Park Lane in the late twentieth century called The Green, which created a village green. During the Second World War, No. 29 Platoon of the Hertfordshire Home Guard was based at the school. Its lieutenant was Maj. Saunders who lived at Park Wood. The former school building is seen from the east.

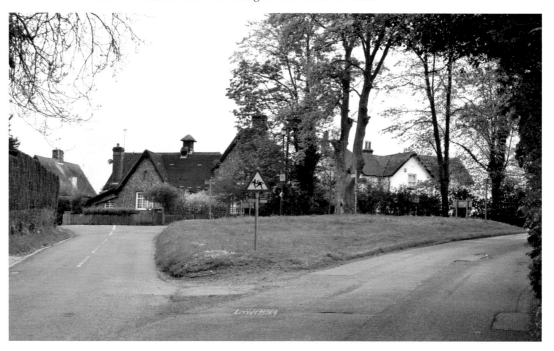

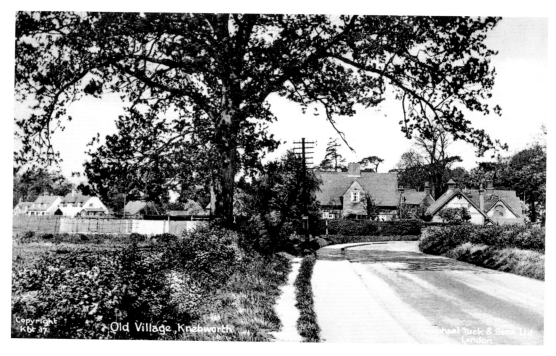

Approaching Old Knebworth; Park Lane
The approach to what has been since 1925 Old Knebworth is seen from Park Lane. The flint-walled school building was built in 1870 and remained a school until 1963, after which it was a nursery school for some years. It is now a private house.

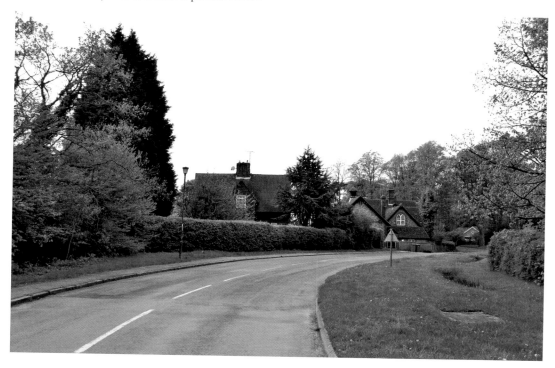

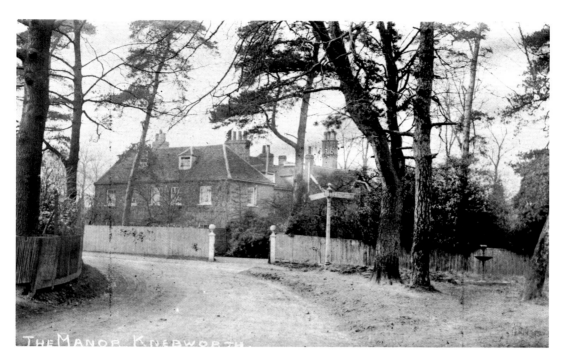

Manor House

Dating from the eighteenth century, the Manor House in Park Lane was extended to the rear in the late nineteenth century. In the 1920s it was the home of Geoffrey Cory-Wright, later the Third Baronet Cory-Wright.

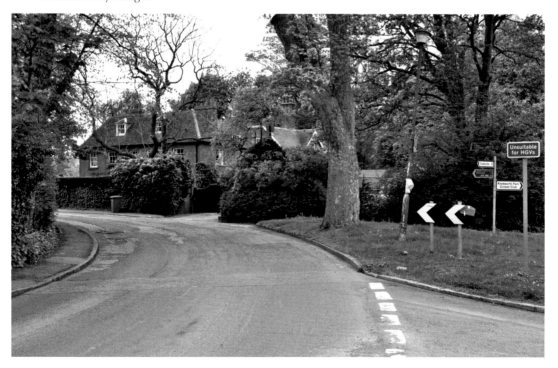

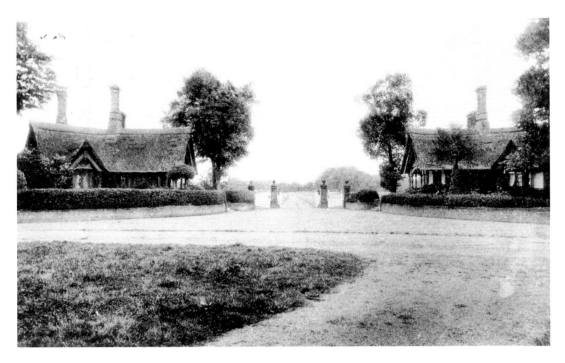

Jubilee Lodges

In 1897, a new entrance to Knebworth Park was constructed from Park Lane, with two lodges (Jubilee Lodges East and West) being built. The original thatched roofs have been replaced, but the chimney stacks with Tudor-style ornamented shafts remain. The war memorial was erected in 1920.

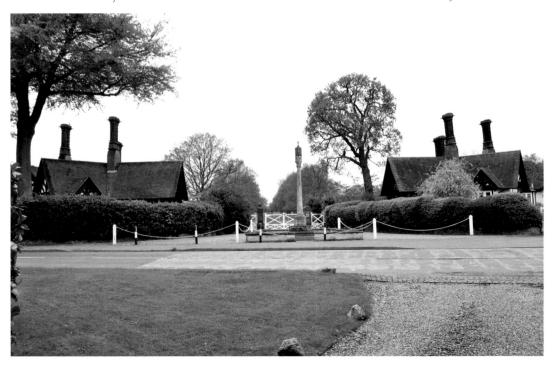

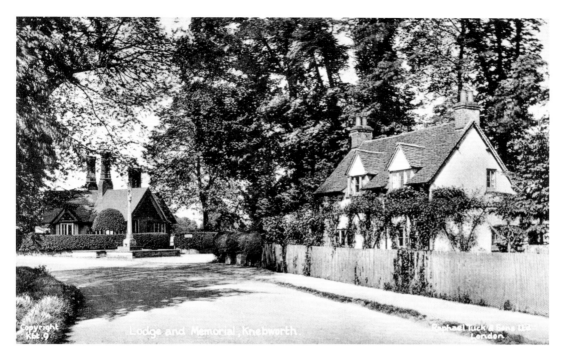

Lodge and Memorial, Knebworth.

Rose Cottage

Rose Cottage, one of relatively few vernacular buildings to remain in Knebworth, stands a few yards east of the Jubilee Lodges. In recent years a development of houses – Manor Farm Stables – has been built on the site of the outbuildings of Manor Farm.

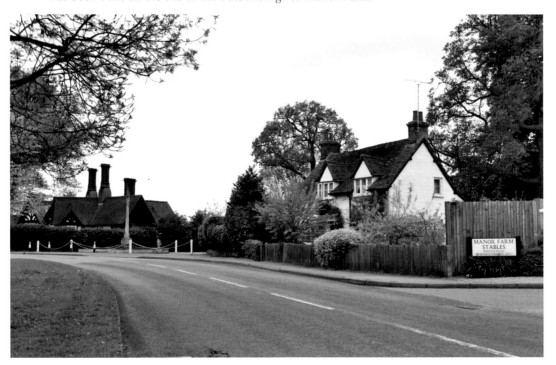

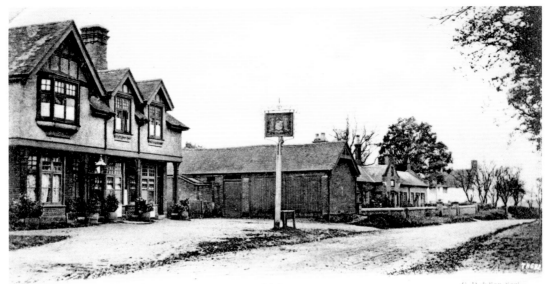

Lytton Arms, Knebworth

W. R. CHORLTON,

Lytton Arms

The current Lytton Arms was built *c.* 1887, replacing an older pub, which still survives as a private house to the left of the photograph, and is now called Old Inn Cottage. The new building was leased by the Knebworth Estate from the outset to the Bishops Stortford brewery of Hawkes & Co., which was taken over by Benskins as long ago as 1898. The Lytton Arms is the only pub to retain an inn sign bracket bearing the 'H. & Co' motif of Hawkes. The almshouses to the right of the Lytton Arms were built in 1836 in gault brick by Elizabeth Bulwer Lytton.

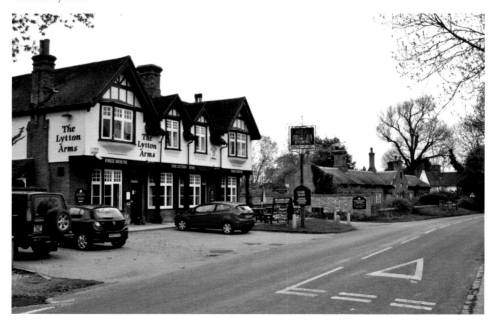

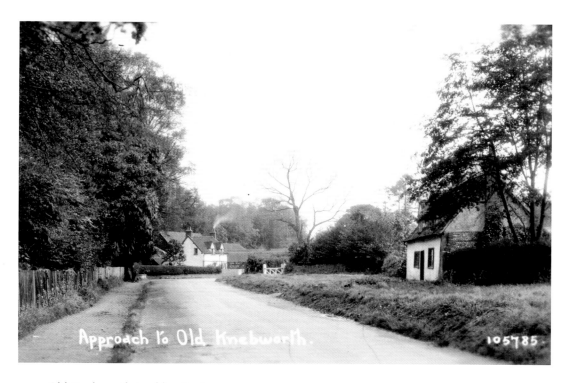

Old Knebworth Looking East

Park Lane looking east, with Manor Gardens Cottage on the right. Another of Old Knebworth's vernacular survivals, this timber-framed building dates from the seventeenth century.

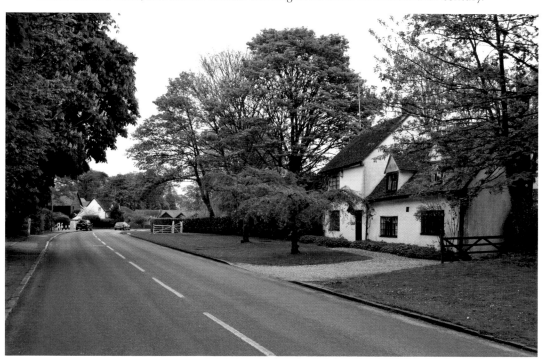

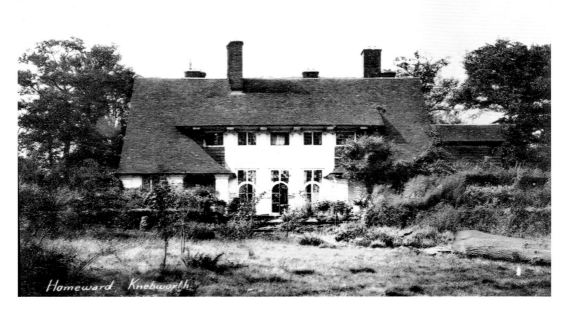

Homewood

Built in 1901 for the Dowager Lady Lytton, to the designs of her son-in-law Edwin Lutyens, Homewood stands at the south of Park Wood off a track that runs from Park Lane called Dowagers Lane. Described as 'a virtuoso display by an expert in three-dimensional form', the house remained in the possession of the Lytton family until 1973. Overlooking the lands of the medieval Great Park, in recent years it offered bed and breakfast accommodation, until late 2010.

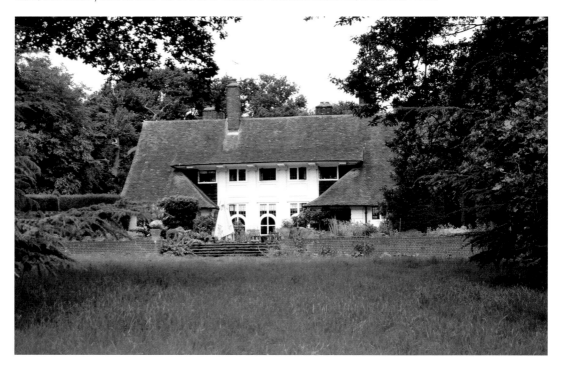

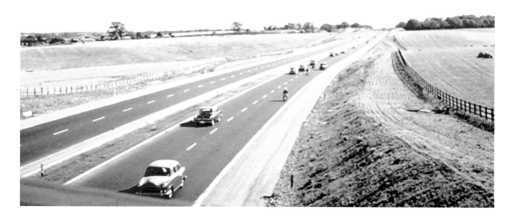

Motorway

Thirty-four years after the A1 was upgraded through Knebworth and Woolmer Green, it was superseded by the A1(M) Stevenage Bypass, which runs from Welwyn to Coreys Mill. The earlier view shows the new motorway on 16 September 1962, the location is the bridge in Park Lane. (John Borne)

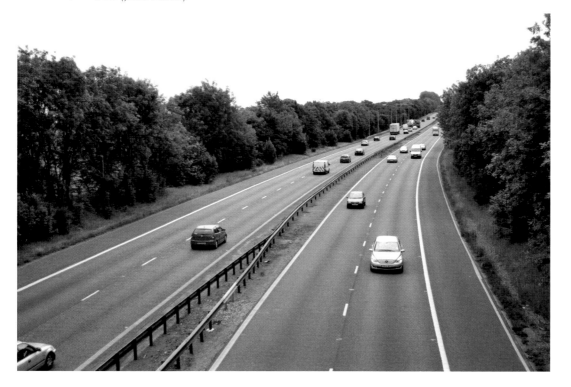

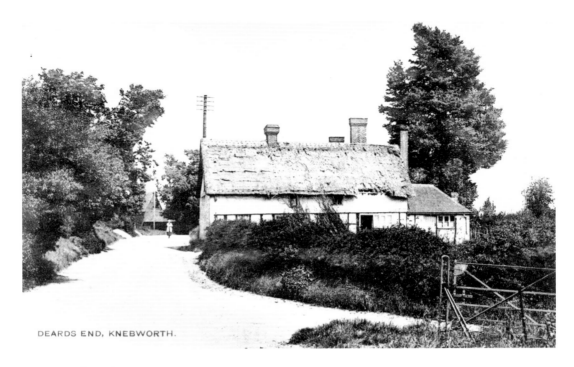

DEARDS END, KNEBWORTH.

Deards End

The family with the longest association with the Knebworth area is the Deards; the first record of a Deards was Robert Derdes in 1339. Members of the family still live locally and before the development of 'New Knebworth' from the 1880s, the only settlement eastwards from what is now Old Knebworth was Deards End. The thatched cottages stood to the west of Deards End Farm on the corner of Gypsy Lane. Their site is now occupied by Deards Cottage, which is at the western end of the Deards End Conservation Area.

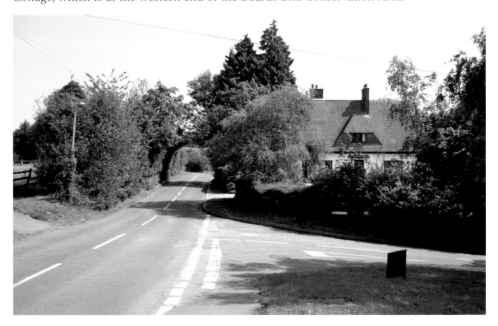

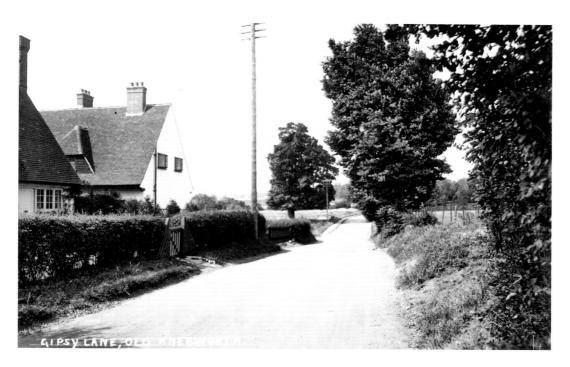

Park Lane, Junction with Gypsy Lane
The view towards Old Knebworth along Park Lane. The turning to the left is Gypsy Lane. In 1901, before the renaming of the 'two Knebworths' to Old Knebworth and Knebworth, Park Lane was called Knebworth Road.

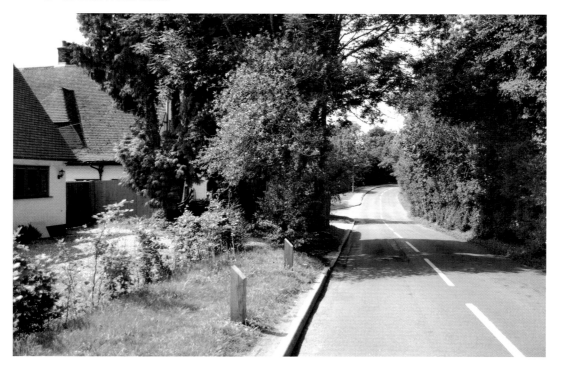

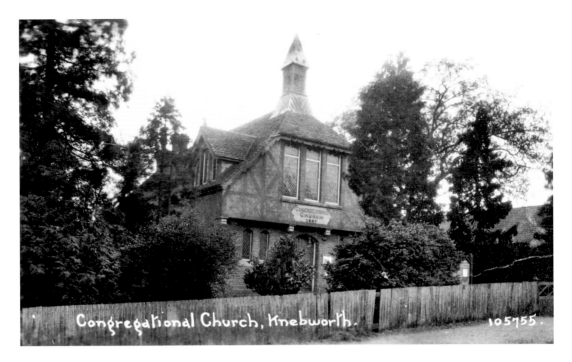

Congregational Church, Knebworth. 105755.

Congregational Church

After a short period when worship was undertaken at the rear of a building in Station Road, Knebworth's congregational church was built in Park Lane in 1887. With seating for approximately 200 people, the church became the Knebworth United Reformed Church in 1973. Since 1996 it has been the home of the Trinity Church union of Knebworth's United Reformed Church and Methodist worshippers. The bell housing was removed in 2003.

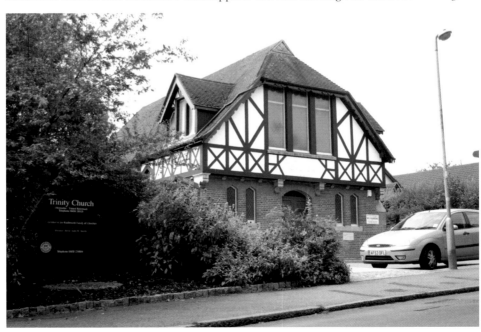

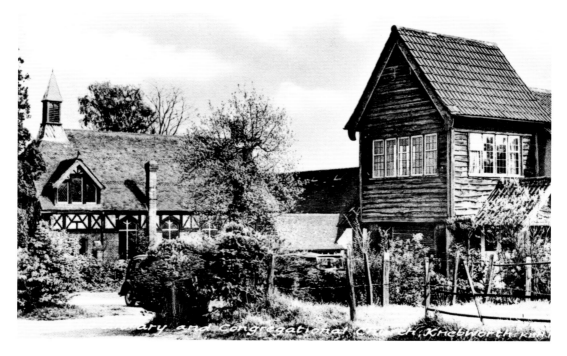

Library and Congregational Church

Knebworth village hall (proper title Knebworth Memorial Hall) was built in 1922. The Knebworth branch of the county library was based in the annex here before being replaced by a mobile library service and then the current library in St Martin's Road in 1970. From 1946 to 1948, films were shown here by the manager of the Pavilion cinema at Welwyn; the closest Knebworth has ever come to having its own cinema.

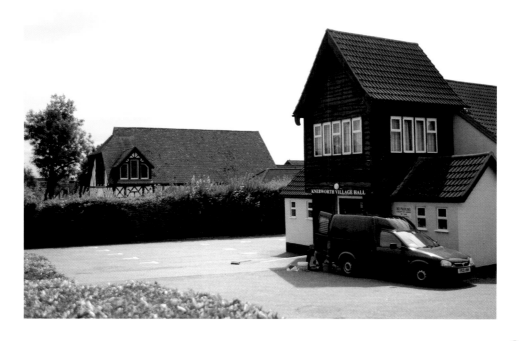

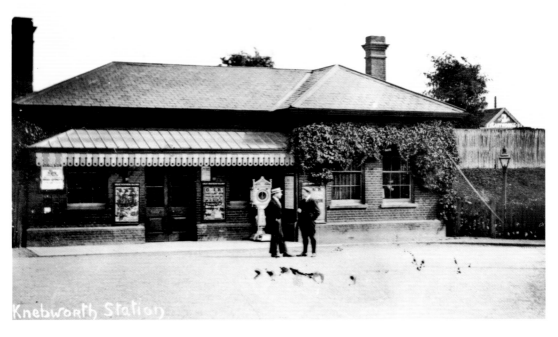

Knebworth Railway Station Frontage
The booking office of Knebworth station, showing the vine that grew up along the frontage. This has long since gone, but the station's other vine, above the stairs to the Down platforms, survived until shortly after the demolition of the platform buildings in 1990.

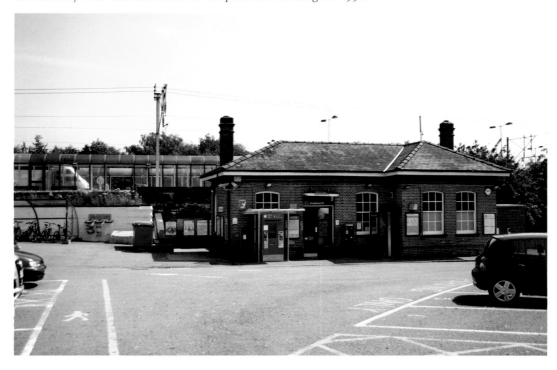

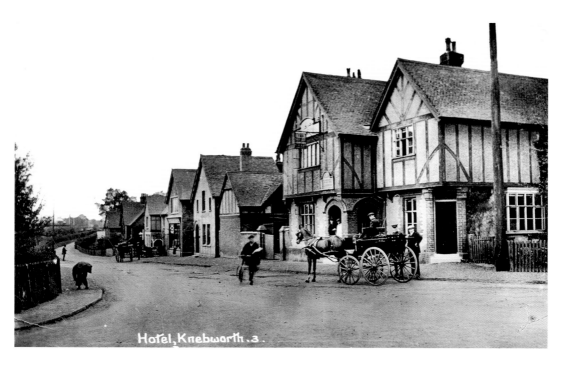

Hotel, Knebworth. 3.

Station Hotel

Built in 1883 and leased to the Ashwell brewery, Fordham & Co., the Station Hotel was completed before the station itself. After a century, it changed its name to the Station pub and is now known as The Station. Many famous musicians played here in the years after the Second World War, including Cleo Laine and Johnny Dankworth and Dudley Moore during his first career as a pianist. Gun Lane, at one time called Mission Road here owing to the Mission Hall, recedes in the distance.

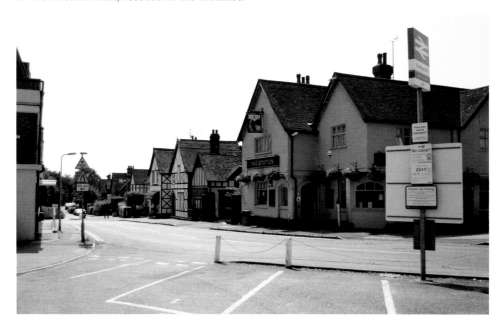

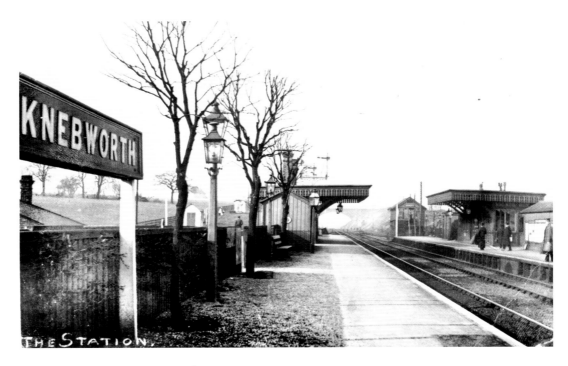

Station Platforms Looking North

Seen from the Down platform, the early view shows the station before the line was widened to its present four tracks. The Down Slow line (serving today's Platform 4) was laid in 1895. In the background can be seen the single-span brick arch of the bridge carrying Deards End Lane across the railway. This is the largest single span on the railway between London and York.

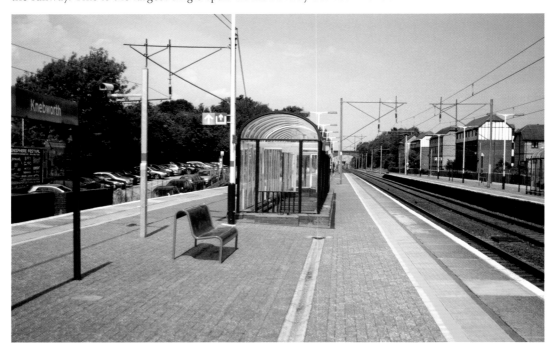

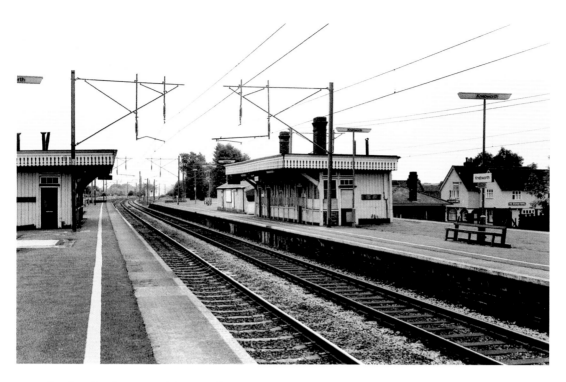

Station Platforms Looking South
The platform buildings at Knebworth station were cleared away and replaced with transparent 'bus shelter' style accommodation in a refurbishment of the station completed in 1990 (John Law).

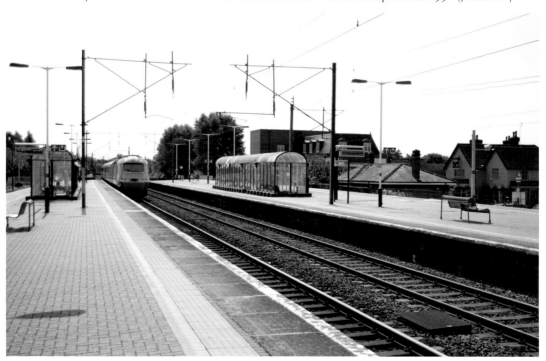

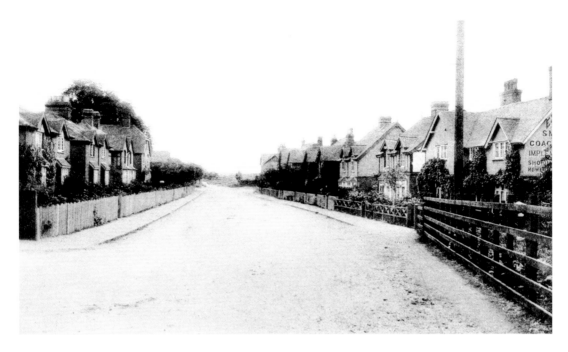

Station Road Looking East

Before the railway came, the lane that is now Station Road ran diagonally through to the kink in Gun Lane visible on page 39. To avoid the need to construct a skew bridge through the railway embankment, the road was rerouted to its present location and, in the early twentieth century, a parade of three shops with flats above was built where the road had been. The westernmost of the three units was the original location of Barclays in Knebworth.

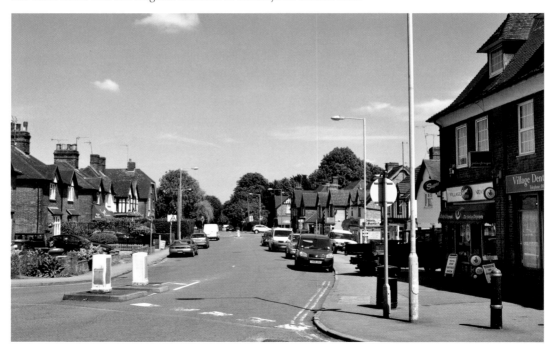

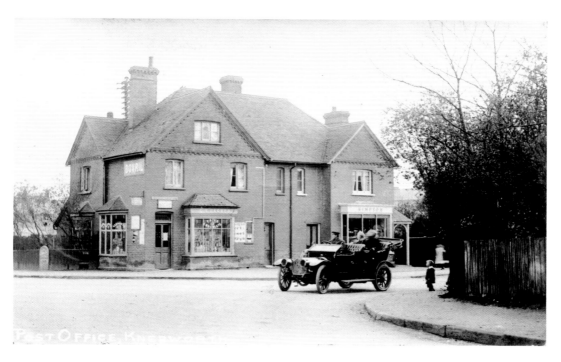

Jacob House, Corner of Station Road

A century ago, when the buildings on the south side of Station Road were still private houses, the only two shops in the street were at the corner with London Road. George Parker's grocer's shop was also New Knebworth's post office, while next door was George Kimpton's bakery.

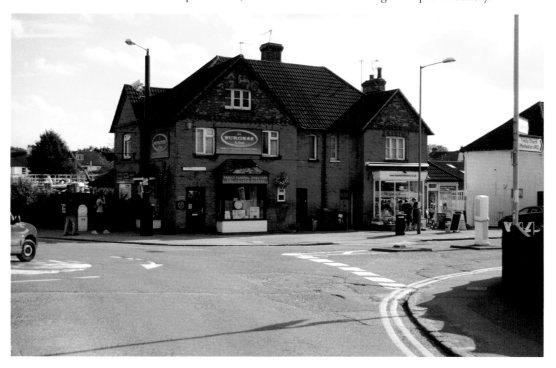

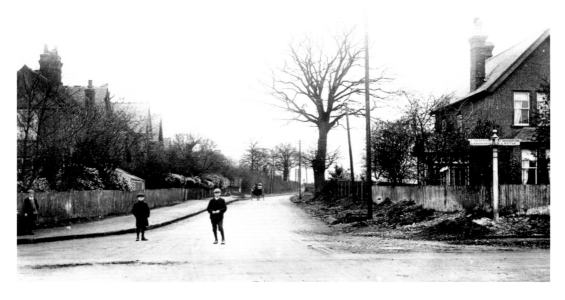

Crossroads Looking North

Originally known as London Road, the main road north towards Broadwater is now Stevenage Road, while the road south of the crossroads continues to be called London Road. After being designated A1 in the roads classification of 1922, it was widened in 1926. The trees of Hopground Spring can be seen on the left-hand side of the road in the middle distance.

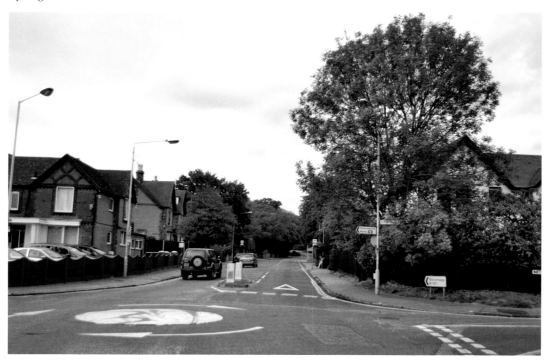

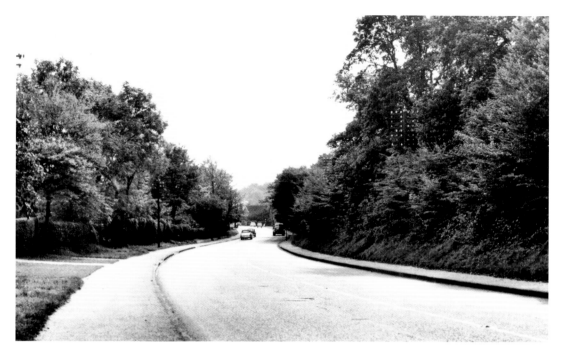

Stevenage Road
The sweep of the 'new' Stevenage Road, looking south towards the crossroads. In the late nineteenth century when it was called London Road, this was little more than a country lane.

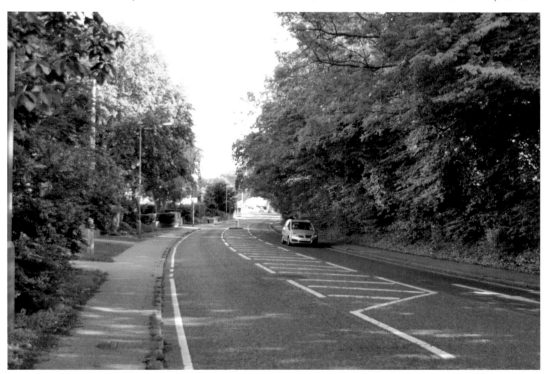

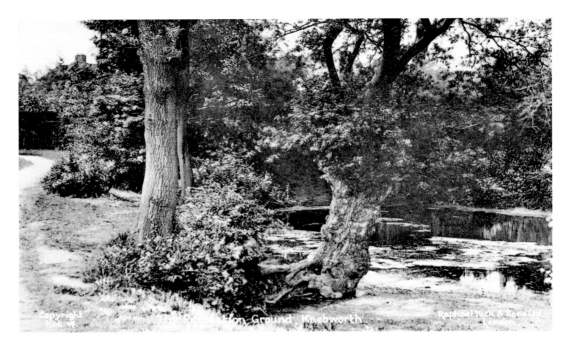

Recreation Ground

The pond in the recreation ground was formerly right on the boundary between the parishes of Datchworth and Knebworth; indeed, maps show the dividing line passing through its middle, which must have presented a dilemma for those 'beating the bounds'. In 1845, it adjoined Oak Tree Common and today is against the rear boundaries of houses in Oakfields Road. The Recreation Ground was opened to the public in 1929.

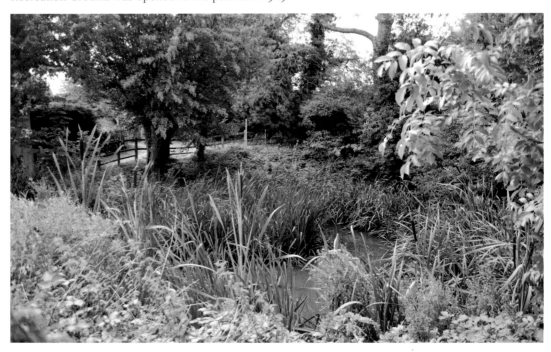

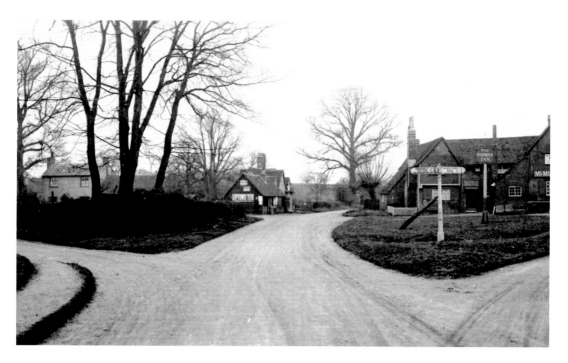

Roebuck

The Roebuck Inn, in the 'vee' between Hertford and London Roads at Broadwater, was formerly in the parish of Knebworth. Today, the parish boundary has moved to follow the Hertford loop line of the railway, a few yards to the west and the Roebuck is in Stevenage

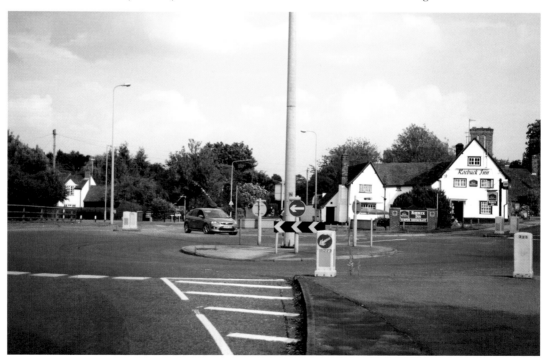

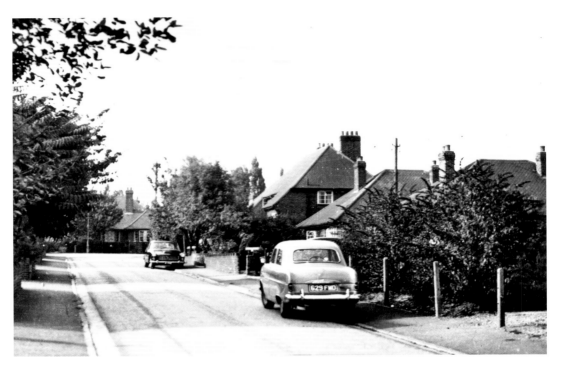

New Close
New Close was laid out to the west of Stevenage Road between the wars, but only the ten houses at its northern end, some of which are seen here, had been built by 1939.

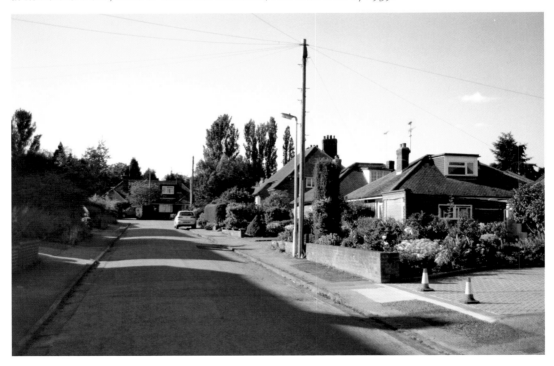

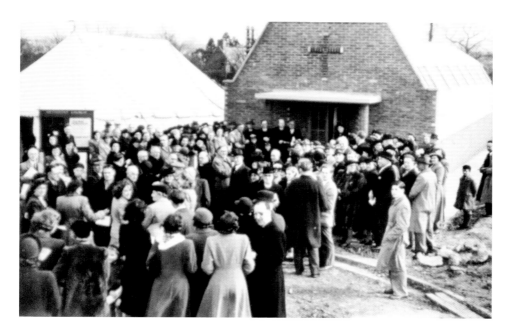

Methodist Church, New Close

Knebworth's Methodist worshippers originally used the mission room in Gun Lane, which before 1915 had been the Anglican church for 'New Knebworth' and is now the site of the British Legion Club. A temporary church was built at the south end of New Close in 1949, which was updated in 1965. With the creation of Trinity church in Park Lane, the New Close church was closed in 1998 and is now the site of Church Close. (Stevenage Museum)

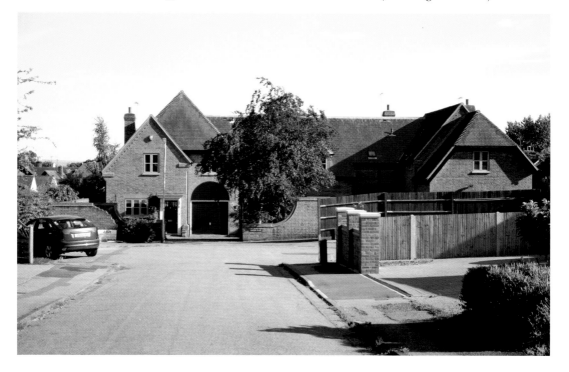

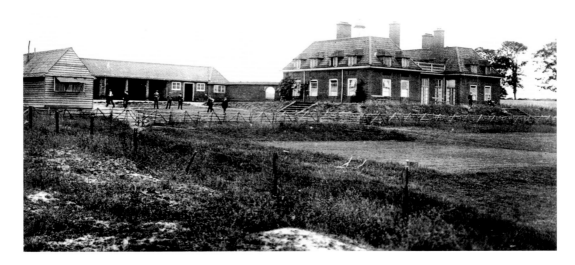

Golf Clubhouse
Replacing the Stevenage Golf Club course at Norton Green, the Knebworth Golf Club was built on land from Broadwater and Deards End farms. Opened in 1908 in the presence of luminaries such as Lord Lytton, former Prime Minister Arthur Balfour and champion golfers James Braid and Harry Vardon, the clubhouse was built to the design of Lutyens. The earlier view shows the wooden caddies' shed and the hurdles required to stop sheep from straying onto the course.

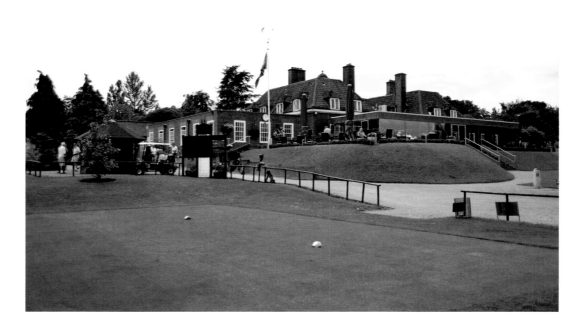

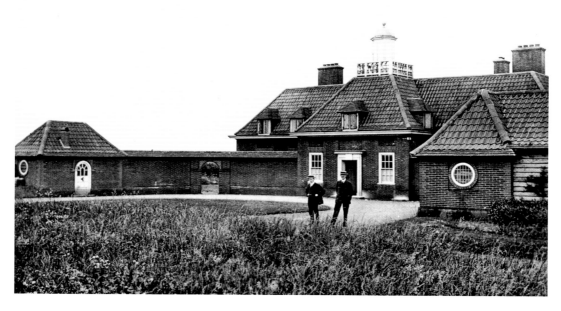

Golf House from the South

The company Knebworth Golf Links Ltd was incorporated in December 1907. A year later, the course and clubhouse (seen here from the south) were complete, £2,000 being allocated for the construction of the former and £3,000 for the latter.

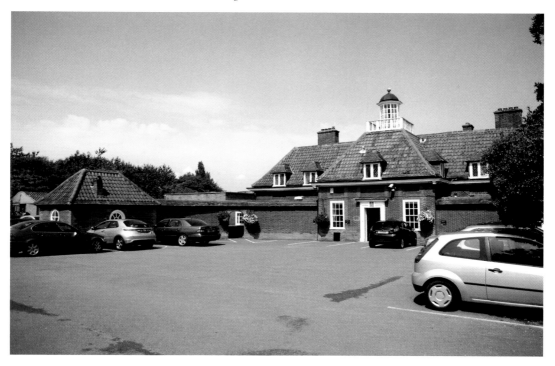

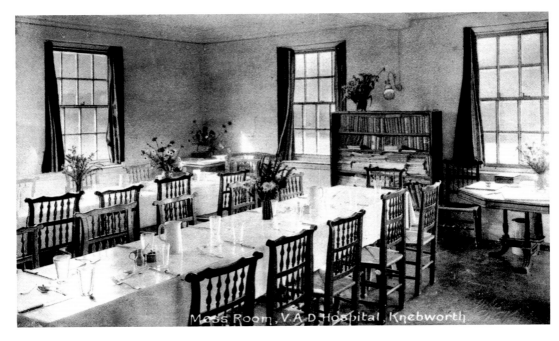

Mess Room, VAD Hospital
During the First World War, the Golf Clubhouse was used as a Voluntary Aid Detachment Hospital under the British Red Cross and the Order of St John. The mess room of the hospital is today the Members' Bar.

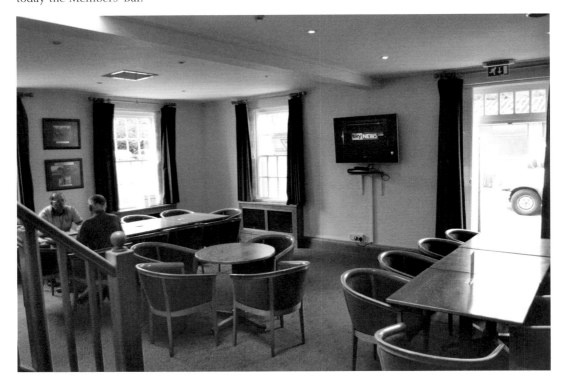

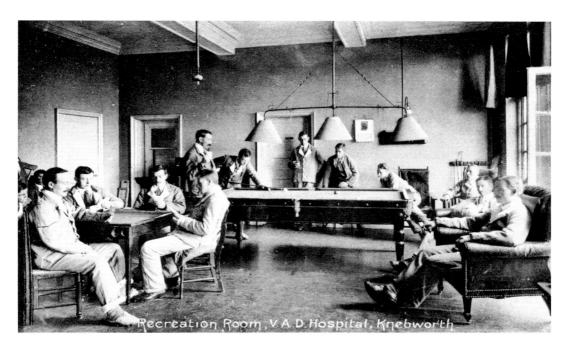

Recreation Room, V.A.D. Hospital, Knebworth

Recreation Room, VAD Hospital

The Recreation Room of the hospital is today's Lounge. Gas lighting had arrived in Knebworth in 1913 with the laying of a main from Welwyn Gasworks. The clubhouse also saw military use during the Second World War, as it was requisitioned in November 1939 and handed back to the club in December 1945.

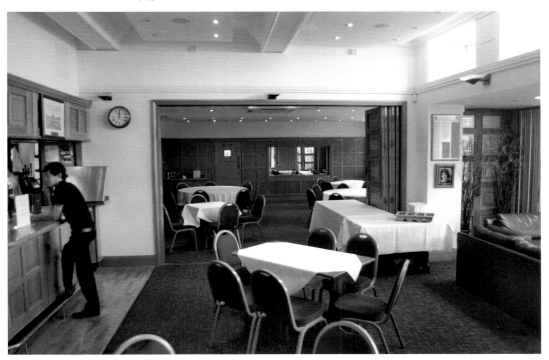

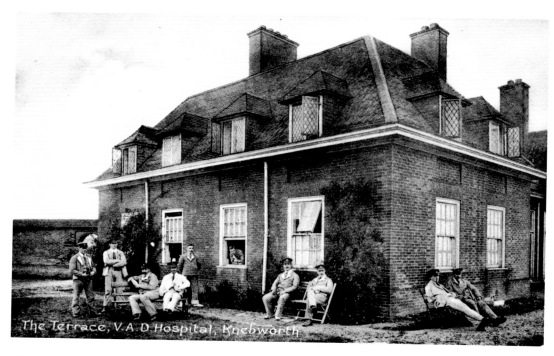

The Terrace, VAD Hospital

Although extensions have been added to Luytens' clubhouse, the 1917 view of service personnel recuperating on the terrace is still readily identifiable. This side of the building was originally the changing room.

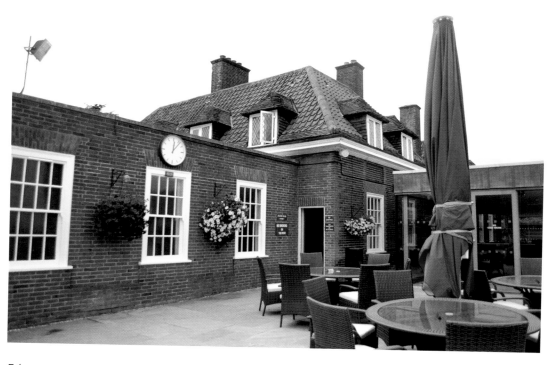

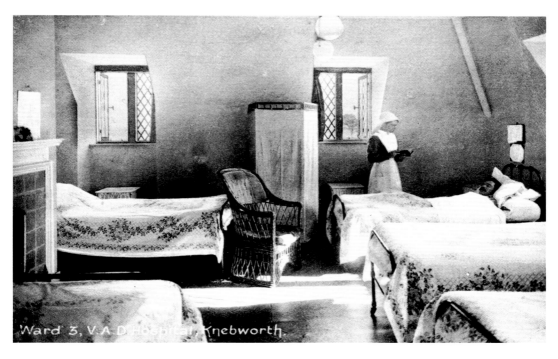

Ward 3, VAD Hospital
After some years as part of the Club Steward's flat, the former Ward 3 of the VAD hospital is today the General Manager's office.

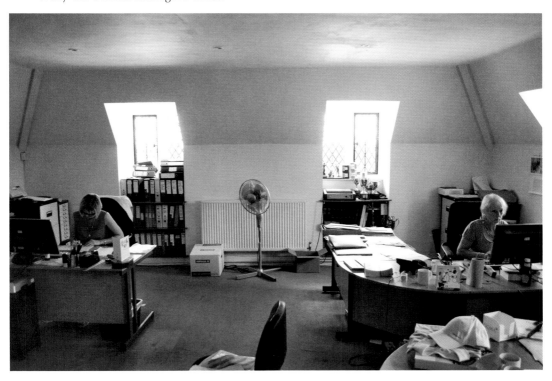

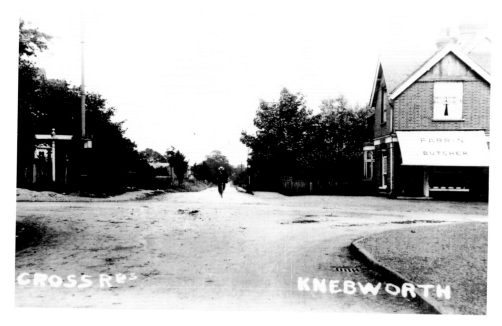

Crossroads Looking East

The crossroads at Knebworth (now a mini-roundabout) dates only back to the late nineteenth century. The eastern arm, Watton Road, was added to what had previously been a T-junction with Station Road, when houses were built eastwards from the main road. The former Farrin's butcher's shop, today thriving as Trussell's, was the first shop to open in London Road and received great prominence in 2003 when it was name checked by Robbie Willams during his record-breaking concerts at Knebworth House. He sang to 375,000 people over three days in what is recognised as the largest musical event ever held in the UK.

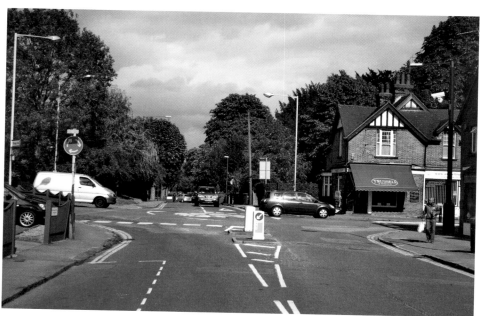

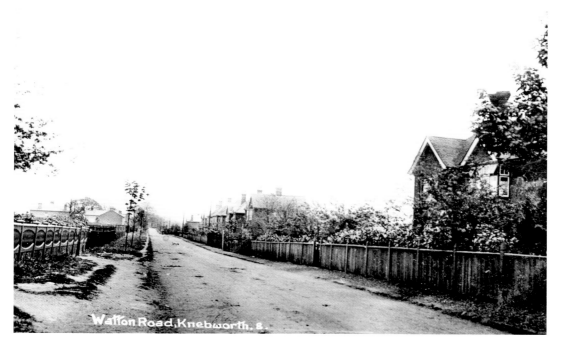

Watton Road
The section of Watton Road built eastwards from what then became the crossroads at the end of the nineteenth century. Grove House, which was home to a private school in the 1920s and 1930s, is seen on the right.

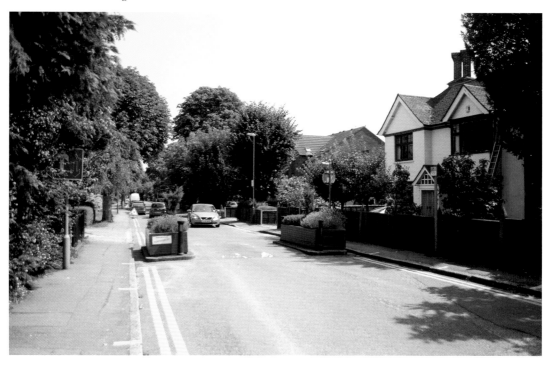

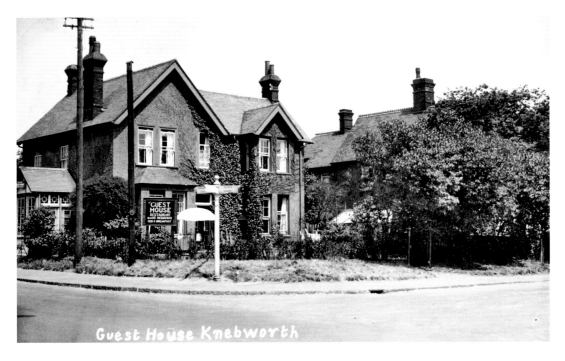

Guest House Knebworth

Guest House
The Station Hotel was not the only place in Knebworth to offer bed and board in the early twentieth century; the house at the corner of Stevenage and Watton Roads traded as the Guest House in the 1930s under the direction of Miss Cole.

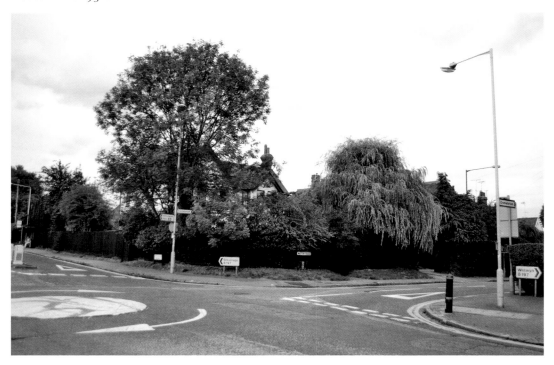

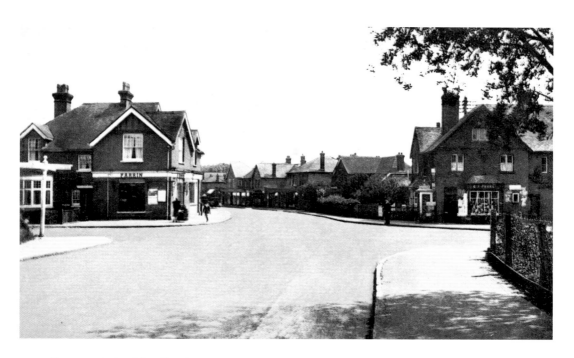

Crossroads Looking South

The section of London Road south of the crossroads. The buildings on the right-hand side of the road stand on what was Hopground Field; a cast-iron milepost marks the fact that the crossroads is 28 miles from London. In the earlier view, Ravenwood house can be seen on the right-hand side of London Road; its site is now the yard of Charles Lowe. Mr Sayer, who lived at Ravenwood, was chairman of the Knebworth parish council twice between 1925 and 1950. He was commemorated by the naming of Sayer Way, off Gun Lane.

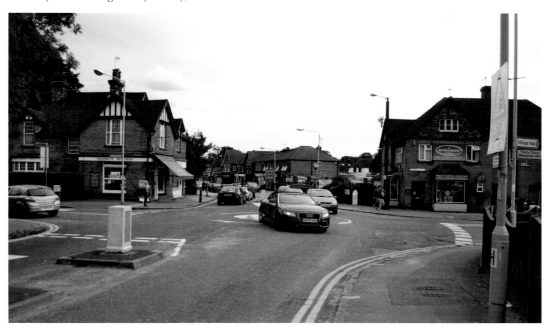

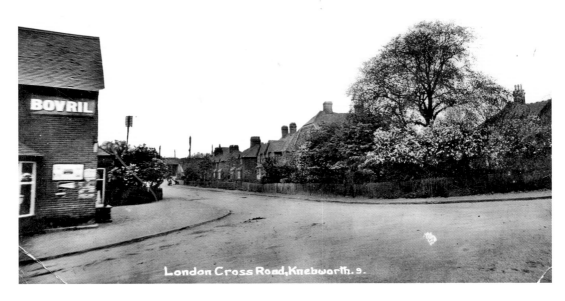

London Cross Road, Knebworth. 9.

Crossroads Looking West

The old lane that became Station Road heads westwards away from London Road/Stevenage Road. In 1900, a bonfire was lit at the crossroads to celebrate the Relief of Mafeking. The village's first telephone box stood beneath the Bovril sign in the 1930s.

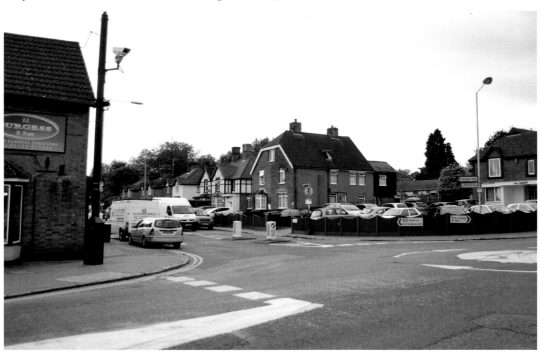

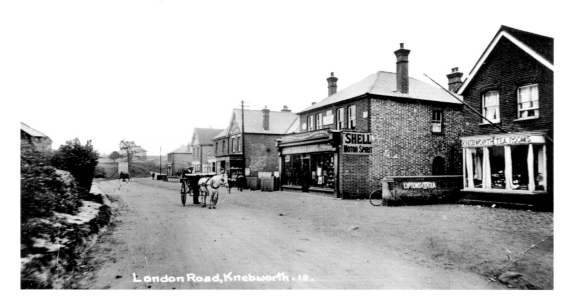

London Road, Knebworth's 'High Street'

Knebworth's *de facto* High Street is the section of London Road between the crossroads and the St Martin's Road/Milestone Road junctions. While the longest-surviving shop is the butcher's, which was the first to be built in London Road (Farrin's, now Trussell's), the longest-surviving business in the ownership of the same family is that of Charles Lowe. A cycle shop at the time of the upper photograph, Lowe's business is today a thriving builders merchants.

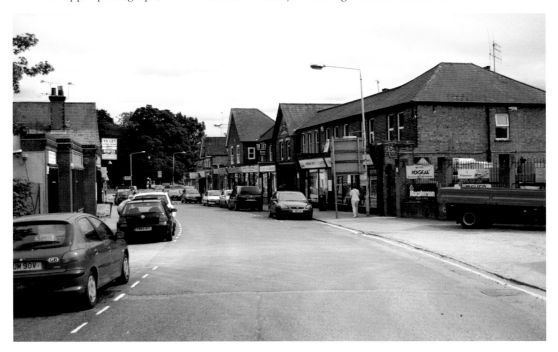

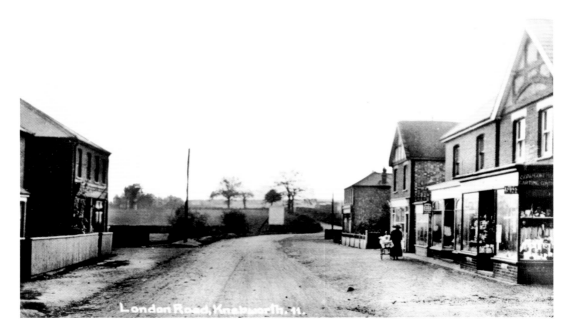

London Road Looking South

An early-twentieth-century view showing, in the middle distance, the empty space where the school would be built. The large house, Pelham Lodge, can just be discerned in the distance between the building and the telegraph pole. This would become the site of the UK's first health farm at the end of the 1950s, started by Leida Costigan. The health farm moved to Henlow Grange in 1961 and the site of Pelham Lodge and its neighbour Warwick Lodge is now the Haygarth development of flats.

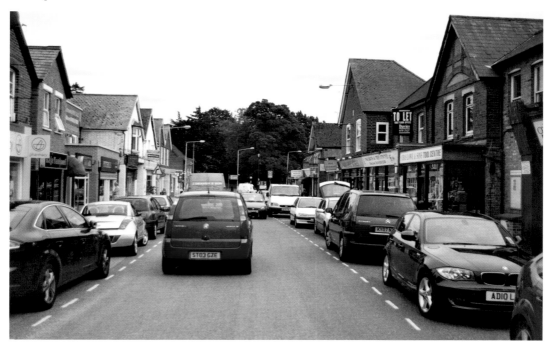

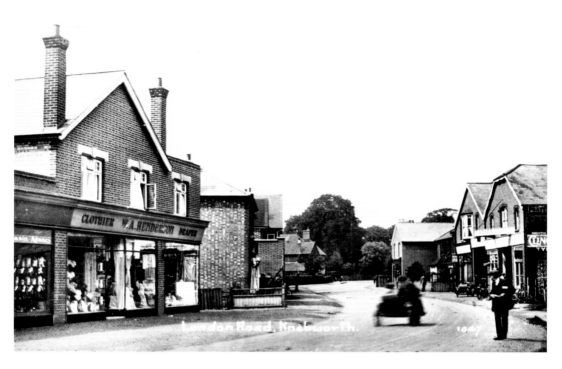

London Road Shops Looking North

A number of concerns with shops in Stevenage had branches in Knebworth. Hendersons, seen in the upper picture, had a department store in Stevenage (and later one in Stevenage's new town centre), while firms such as Horsnell's the confectioner, Thody the butcher and Kimpton's the baker were also represented in Stevenage. Today the pattern continues with funeral directors Austin's of Letchmore Green, Stevenage, having a branch in Knebworth and Stevenage barber's *Boys 2 Men* also having a shop in London Road.

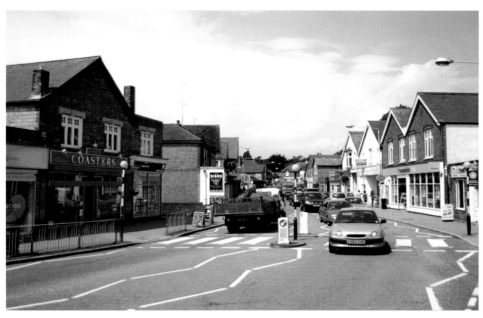

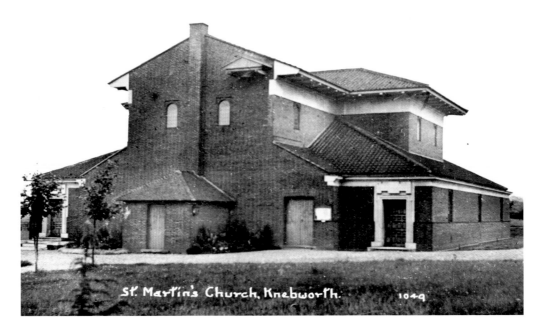

St Martin's Church

St Martin's church was built on the plot of a house whose builder had gone bankrupt before completion. The watercolour shows the church as planned by Lutyens. In the event (and in common with all of Lutyens' other ecclesiastical designs, including Liverpools' Roman Catholic Cathedral), St Martin's was not completed as Lutyens intended. When the church was consecrated in 1915, its western end was finished with a temporary plain brick wall, which remained until the church was finished in 1964 with a revised west end designed by Sir Albert Richardson.

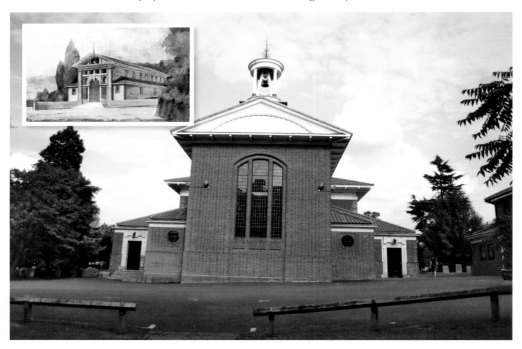

Swangleys Lane

There was a farm at Swangleys as far back as 1278; the farmhouse seen in the earlier view, concealed by trees in the 2011 picture, dates from the nineteenth century. In common with other farms in Knebworth, Swangleys was tenanted by a Scottish farmer (Samuel Wallace from Lanarkshire) in the years after the poor harvests of the 1870s and early 1880s when local tenants first obtained rent reductions and then left their farms.

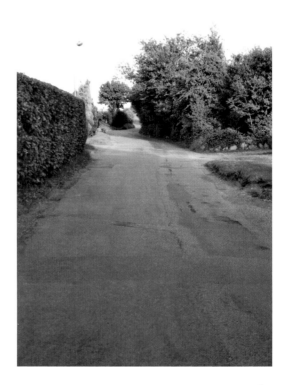

SWANGLEYS LANE, KNEBWORTH.

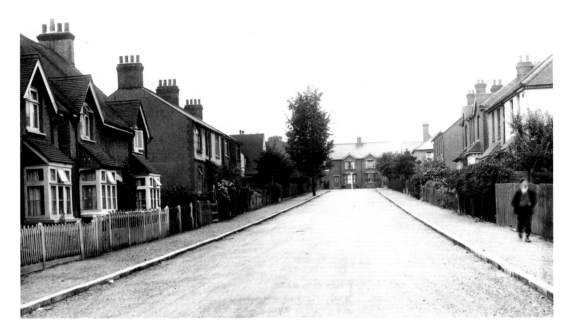

Milestone Road
Linking London Road to Pondcroft Road, Milestone Road was one of the first three roads in Knebworth to have its houses numbered, along with Station Road and Pondcroft Road, around 1924. It is built on what was part of the Hopground Field.

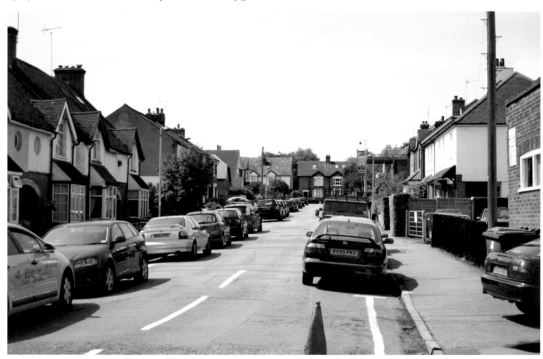

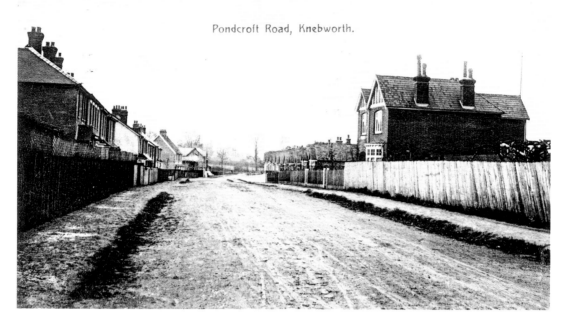

Pondcroft Road, Knebworth.

Pondcroft Road
Looking south along Pondcroft Road, which was laid out just before the Garden Village plan was drawn up. The six dwellings of The Bungalows, seen on the right-hand side of the street, were built during the First World War and originally numbered separately, but are now Nos 56–66 Pondcroft Road.

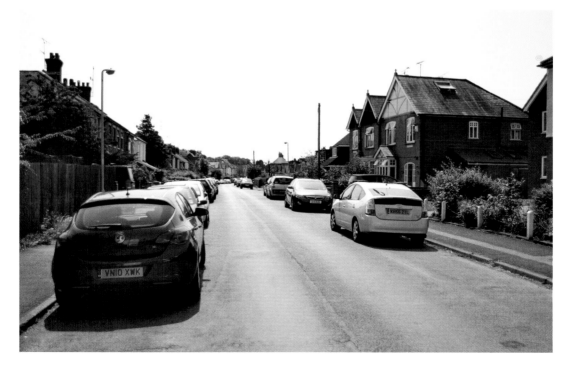

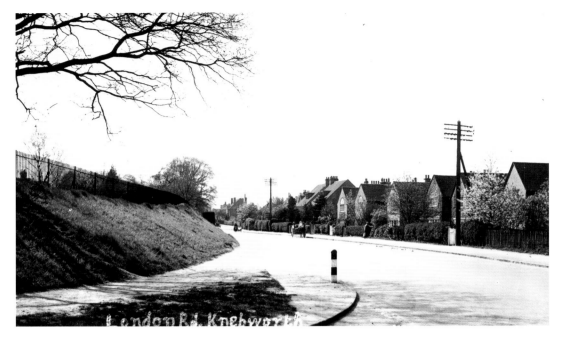

London Road by the School
London Road looking south from the junction with Swangleys Lane. In the distance of the earlier view, the high roof of the house that became the Presbytery of the St Thomas More Roman Catholic church. This was built in 1935 as a temporary building; a larger, impressive church, was built in the space between the two in 1962.

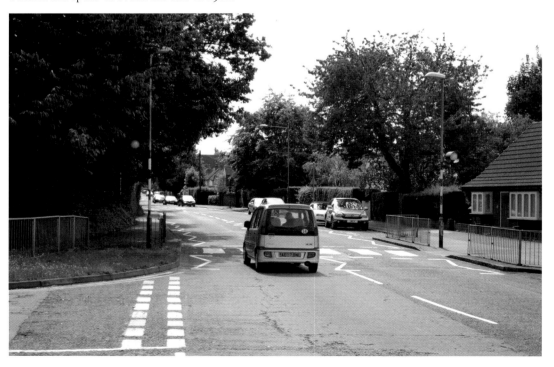

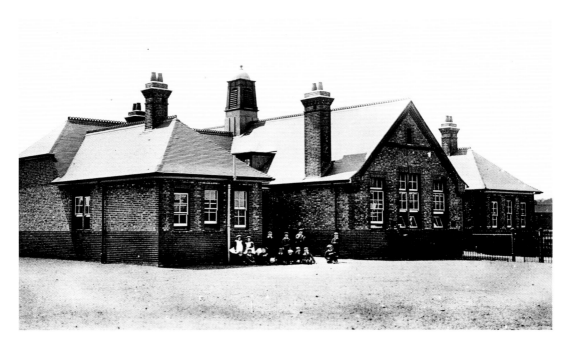

Knebworth School

Built by Hertfordshire county council in 1912 on a piece of land formerly known as Gravelly Hill, Knebworth school has been extended several times since. Secondary education has always been provided by the schools of Stevenage and Hitchin, although in recent years there have been proposals to build a secondary school in Knebworth or Woolmer Green. However, in May 2011 the government rejected the proposal for an 800-pupil school.

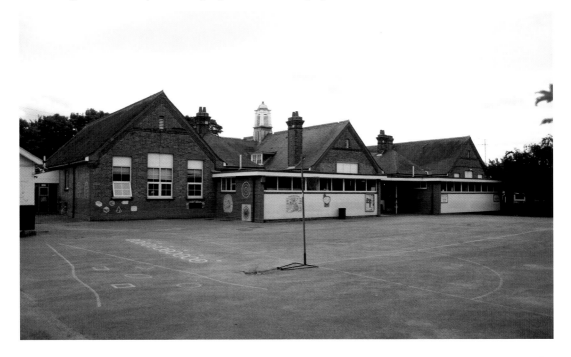

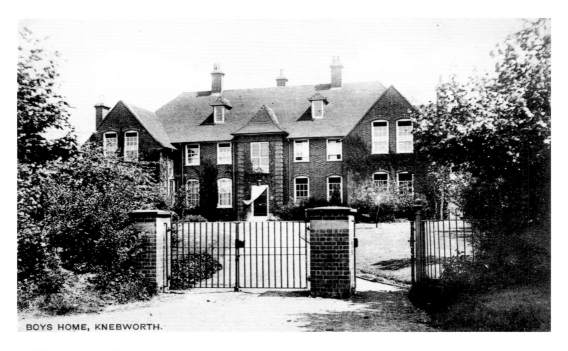

BOYS HOME, KNEBWORTH.

St Alban's Home For Boys

Founded at Rectory Cottage in 1888 – at the corner of Old Knebworth and Park Lanes – and known as the Knebworth Cottage Home, the Knebworth Home for Boys expanded into new premises in London Road in 1914, at which time it took the name St Alban's Home for Boys. The new building was designed by E. J. May and could accommodate up to forty boys; it closed in 1975 and is now Stepping Stone Preschool nursery.

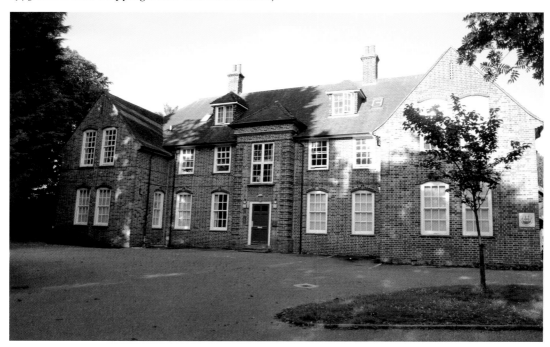

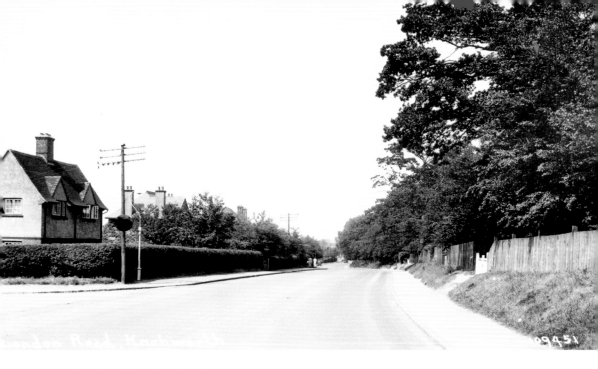

London Road Looking North
The view north along London Road from the junction with Gun Road. The trees on the right are the remains of Pullins Spring, a small wood which separated the road from the Great Pullards field.

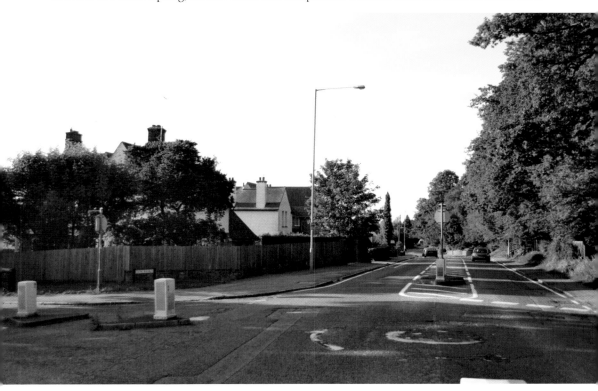

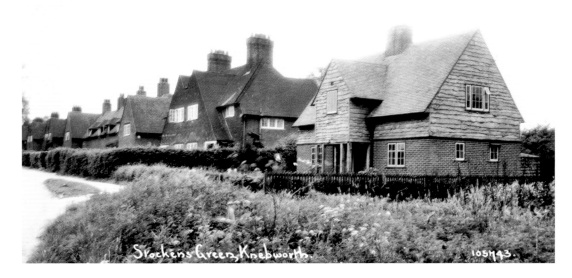

Stockens Green

Only two roads on the estate plan drawn up for the Garden Village were actually constructed – Oakfields Road and Stockens Green, seen here. The latter was the location of cottages built to the designs of Pepler & Allen of Croydon and Courtenay Crickmer, who had worked on Letchworth Garden City from 1907. The first sod of Knebworth Garden Village was cut here in a ceremony in 1912. The houses were let by a co-partnership tenant society, called Knebworth Tenants Ltd, which still maintains forty-two houses in what is now the Stockens Green Conservation Area. The Conway Commercial School was at 28 Stockens Green in the 1930s.

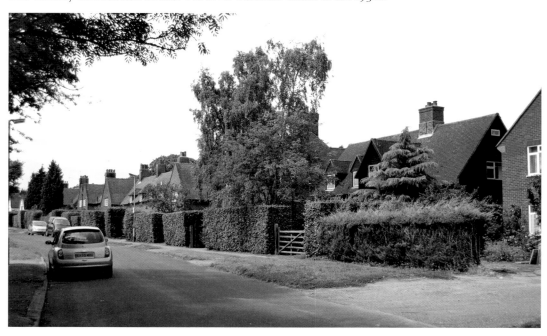

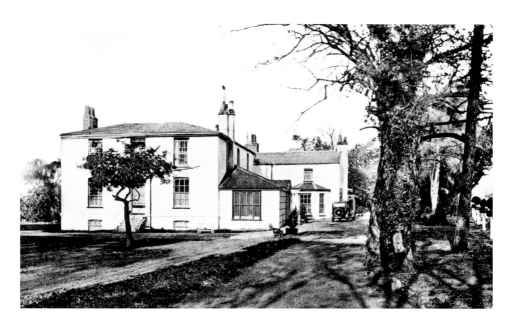

Great North Road Hotel

Gun Lodge, a large house on London Road, at the south of what would become 'New Knebworth', was the first building to be erected at the roadside between Woolmer Green and Broadwater. Extant in the 1870s, it became the Great North Road Hotel in the 1930s and after fire damage was closed in the early 1970s. A riding school continued in the barns to the rear for some years, but eventually the building was demolished. The nursing home Monread Lodge occupies the land immediately to the south of the old building; the site of the hotel itself is now a dense thicket. One squat brick pier and the dropped kerbs marking the 'in and out' access to the hotel remain on the pavement of London Road as a marker of its former presence.

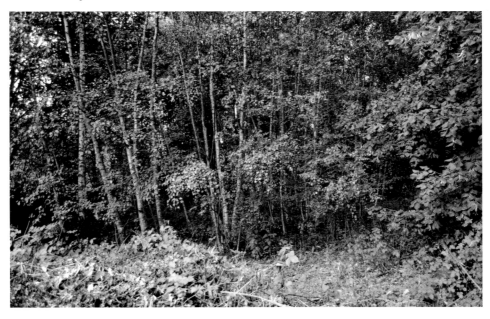

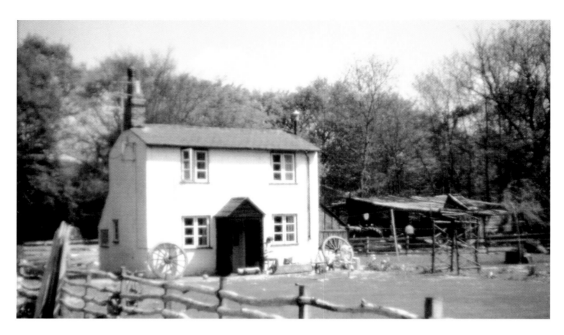

Pigeonswick

The delightfully named Pigeonswick Cottage is at the northern edge of the parish of Knebworth and is accessed by road south of Stevenage via Norton Green. Here fences are manufactured using the timber from the adjoining woods of the Knebworth Estate. (Stevenage Museum)

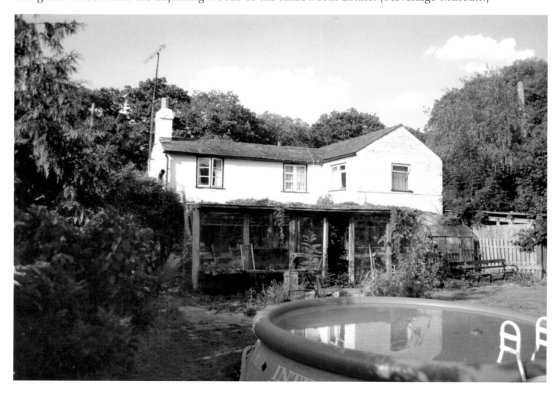

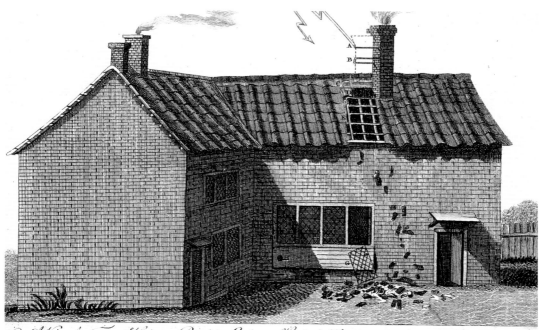

A View of a Farm House at Rasling End, near Hitchin in Hartfordshire, Struck by Lightning June 26.th 1771

Rustling End Farm

A large part of the parish of Knebworth is to the west of the Old London Road (Welwyn–Hitchin). Rustling End Farm, part of the Knebworth estate until 1977, a timber-framed house clad by later brickwork, is seen first after being struck by lightning in 1771.

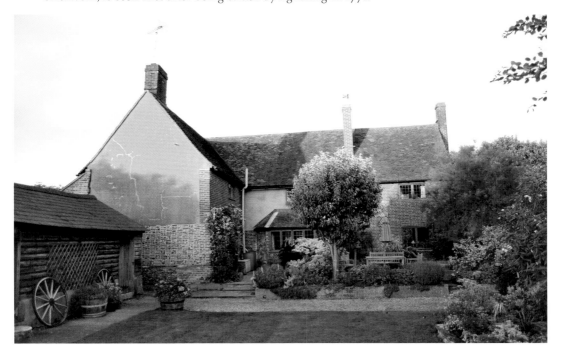

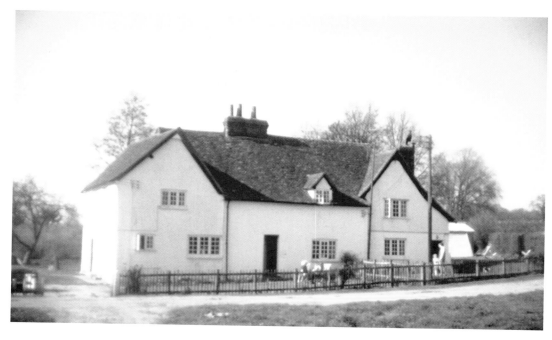

Rye End Cottages

At the south-western edge of the parish of Knebworth, two and a half miles from St Mary's church, the parish boundary follows the line of a Roman road from Verulamium to Baldock. The water mill here is long gone, but the listed cottages here, dating back in part to the 1500s, remain. (Stevenage Museum)

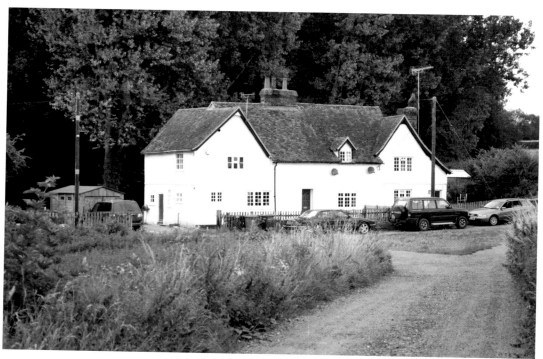

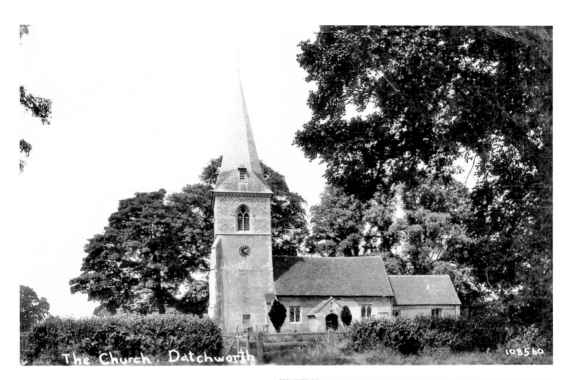

The Church, Datchworth

Datchworth Church

Datchworth church, dedicated to All Saints, is a prominent local landmark at 404ft above sea level. The spire was added to the fifteenth-century tower in 1875, at the same time as the clock was installed in memory of former rector William Williamson.

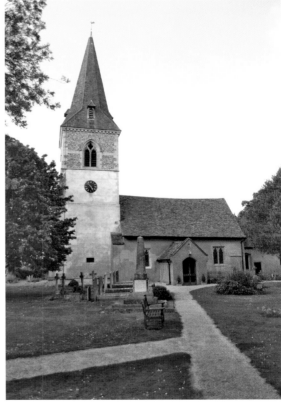

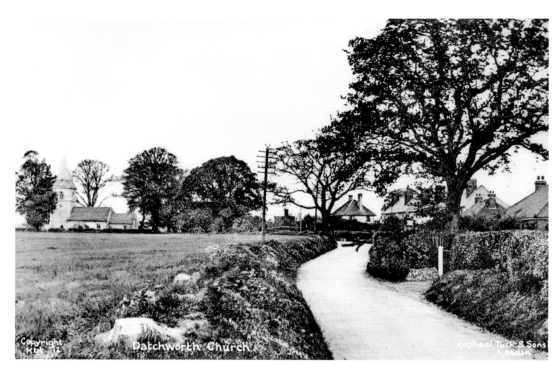

Datchworth Church from Bury Lane

The first council houses in Datchworth are seen here in Bury Lane. They were built in 1921. Electricity followed eight years later, supplied by the North Met power company.

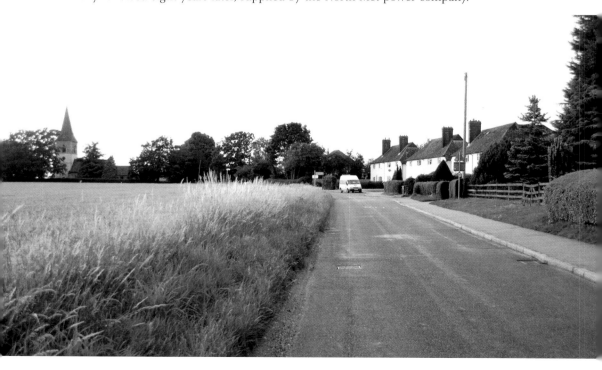

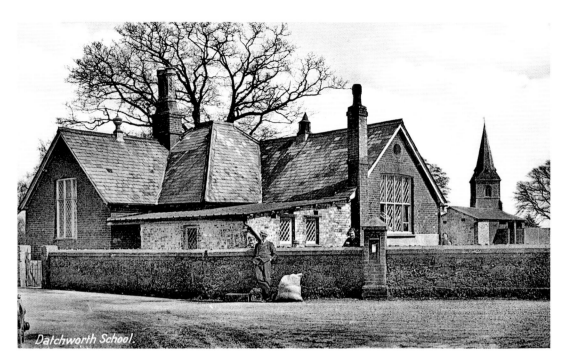

Datchworth School.

Datchworth School

All Saints Church of England (Voluntary Aided) primary school dates back to 1820, fully fifty years before the Elementary Education Act of 1870 made compulsory the provision of schooling for children between the ages of five and twelve. It has had to be extended in 1859, 1961, 1969, 1972 and 2003 as the village of Datchworth has expanded.

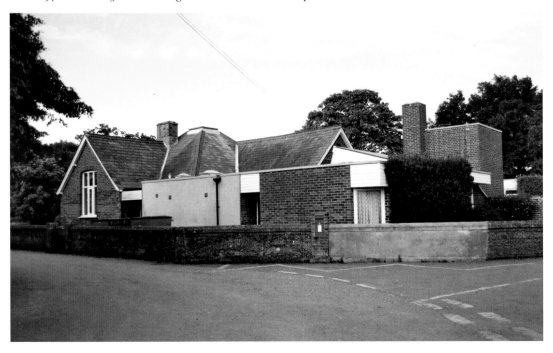

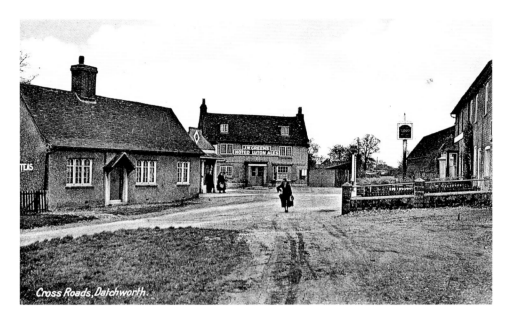

Datchworth Crossroads

With two pubs and shops, the commercial centre of Datchworth is around the crossroads at Datchworth Green. The Tilbury pub at the corner of Watton Road, known as the Tilbury Fort in the nineteenth century, faces the camera, while the inn sign of the Plough, once an outpost of Wright's Brewery of Walkern, can be seen on the right. The 'Teas' sign advertises the refreshment rooms of Mrs Buckridge, which flourished in the 1930s.

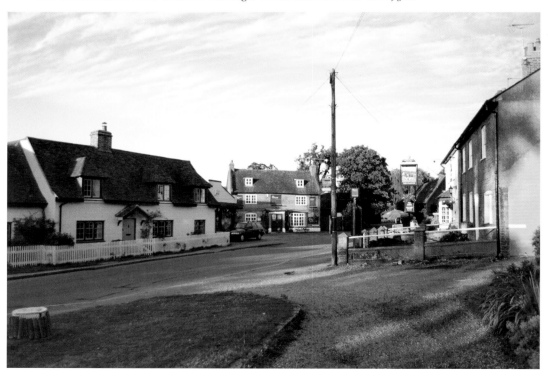

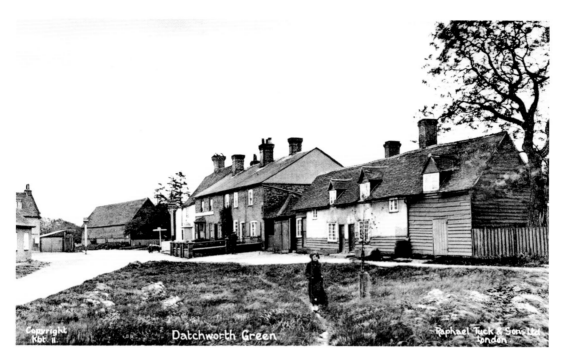

Datchworth Green

Copyright Kbt. II.

Raphael Tuck & Sons Ltd London

Datchworth Green Looking East
The large barn of Hoppers Hall Farm can be seen opposite the Tilbury in Watton Road; today this has been converted into a house. In the earlier view, Mark Miller's blacksmith shop is at the right-hand end of the slate roofed cottages (No. 9 Datchworth Green). Today this is the location of Datchworth Museum.

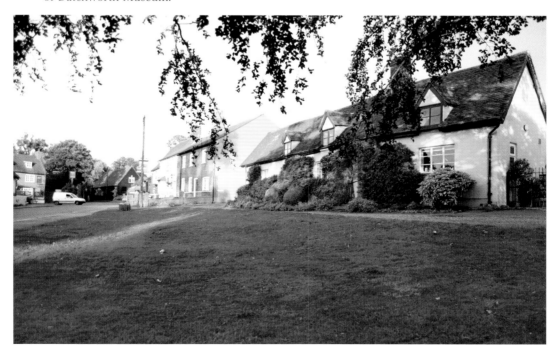

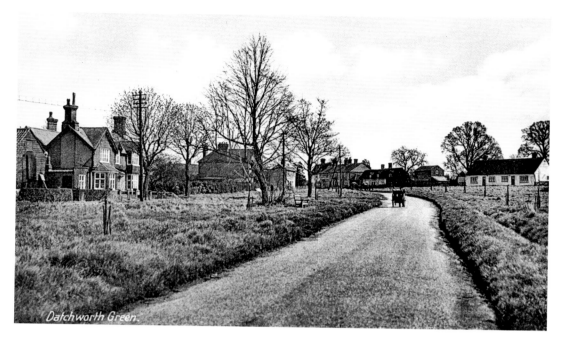

Datchworth Green

The open expanse of Datchworth Green was the subject of a pioneering Village Improvement Scheme, which was completed in 1937, providing a sports pavilion, children's playground and tennis courts, as well as improving the cricket pitch. The avenue of flowering cherry trees, planted to mark the Silver Jubilee in 1935, has also changed the character of the green, the trees being seen soon after planting in the earlier view. The very last enemy action on British soil during the Second World War occurred on 29 March 1945 when the last V1 'doodlebug' to reach British land fell near Datchworth Green.

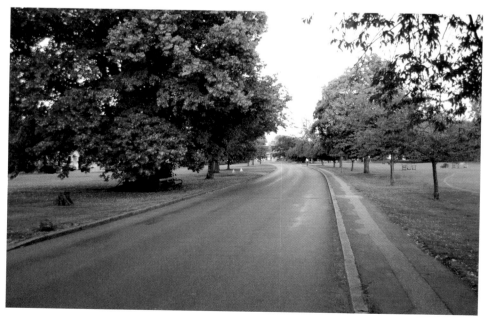

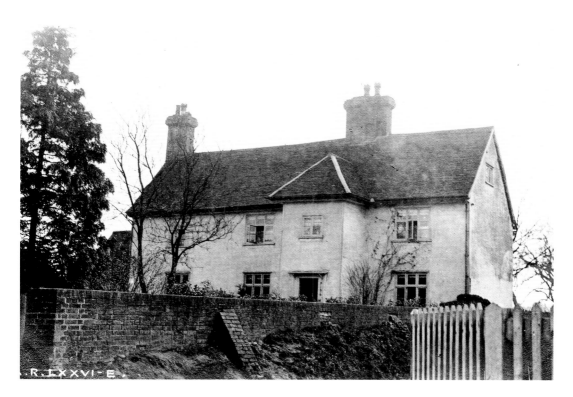

Datchworth, Hoppers Hall

Built around 1640, Hoppers Hall is a large timber-framed house that was formerly a farm, run for much of the twentieth century by the Little family. In 1926, two acres of the Orchard Field at the rear were sold to Alan Silver Woodthorpe of Mardley Hill for £200, on which Orchard House has now been built.

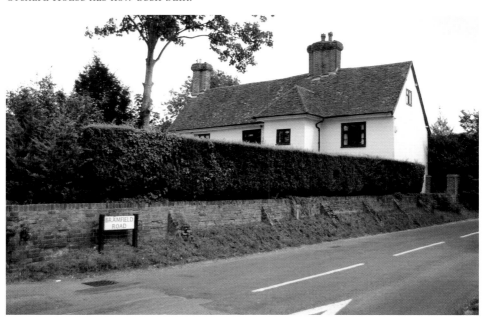

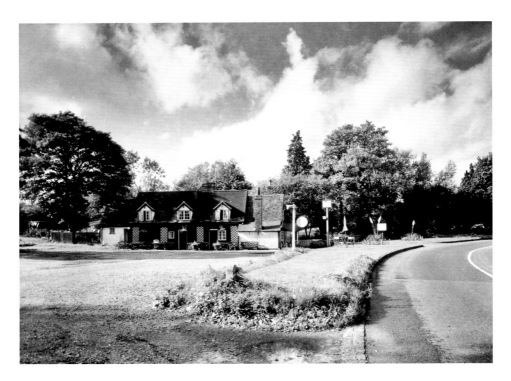

Chequers Bragbury End

The hamlet of Bragbury End was formerly at the north-east corner of the parish of Datchworth, and is now part of the Borough of Stevenage. The Chequers public house, owned by the brewers Christy of Hoddeson in the nineteenth century, is today part of the Vintage Inns chain. It remained lit by oil lamps until the 1950s. (Stevenage Museum P3737)

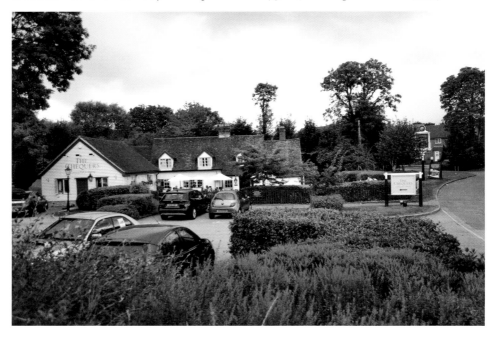

Bulls Green, the Horns

Once a tied house of the old Lucas Brewery of Hitchin, the Horns dates back to the sixteenth century. The nineteenth-century extension to the right was built as a dairy. In 1782, the body of the notorious footpad Walter Clibbon was brought here for inquest after he was shot during an attempted robbery. Some accounts of the demise of Walter Clibbon state that his body spent the night in the barn at the Horns; whether it was the attractive thatched barn, which was photographed in the car park in 1975, is unclear, but with non-domestic thatched buildings becoming very rare in Hertfordshire, its loss in recent years is to be lamented. (Stevenage Museum)

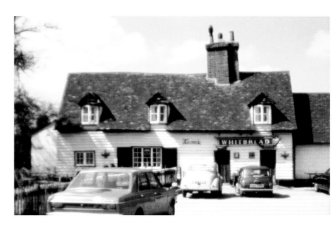

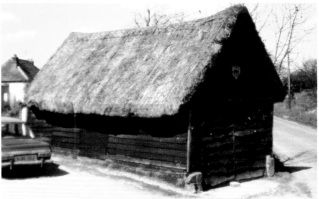

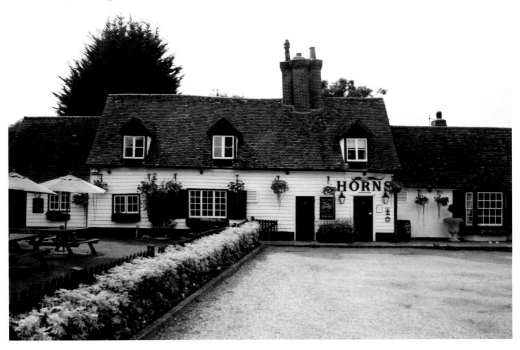

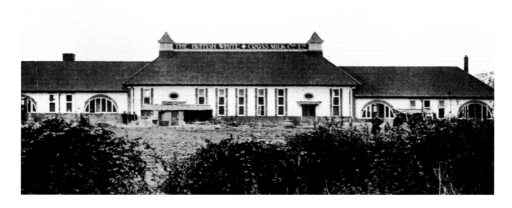

Woolmer Green White Cross Factory

A major part of the Garden Village plan for Knebworth was the establishment of the White Cross condensed milk factory at Woolmer Green. Opened by the Countess of Lytton in 1908, the enterprise, screened from London Road by a plantation of pine trees, lasted until the mid-1930s when it was replaced by the works of the Allied Guano & Chemical Company, which made artificial fertilisers. Subsequently, it was the location for Trubro, which made the materials to stiffen shirt collars, and Almco Supersheen, where machines for cleaning castings were manufactured. It has been the premises of Entech (Environmental Technology) since 1981, which specialises in the design, manufacture and installation of innovative building components.

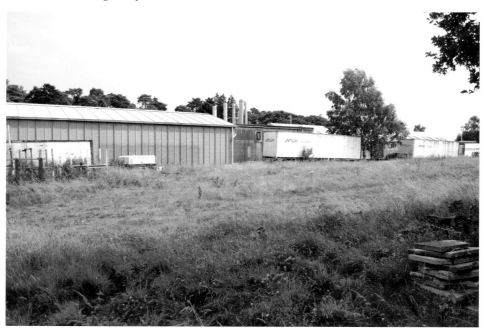

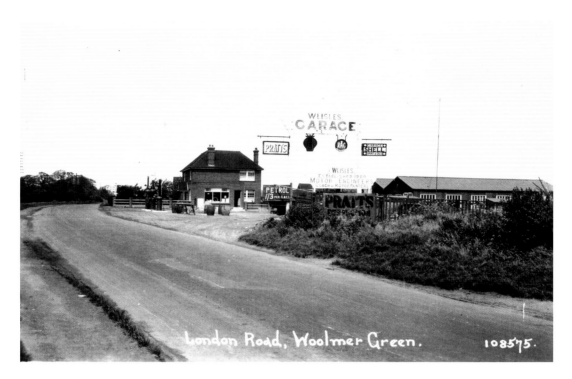

London Road, Woolmer Green. 108575.

Woolmer Green Lisles

The engineering and motor business of William Lisles was founded in 1900. From 1939 it was owned by a member of the Deards family who had commenced work here as an apprentice in 1917. It is now part of the Marshall group of garages. Following the closure of Woolmer Green's post office, grocer, baker and butcher in the last few decades of the twentieth century, the Spar shop at the garage is now the 'village store' for Woolmer Green.

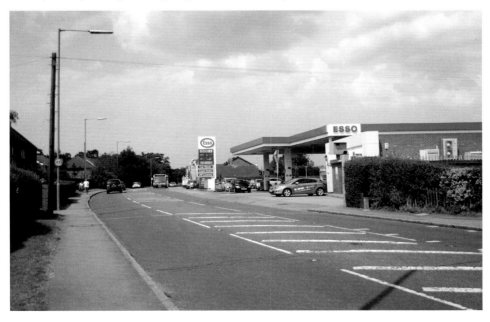

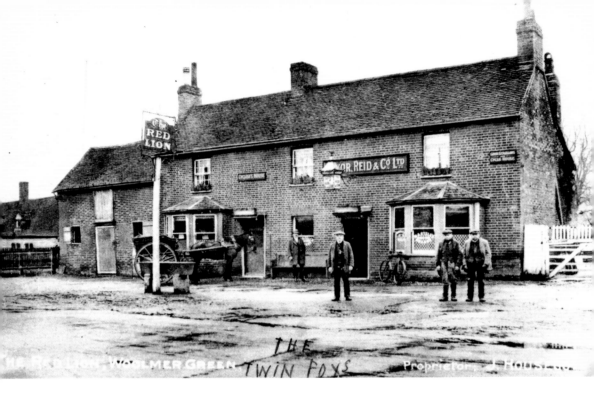

Woolmer Green Red Lion

A century separates these two images of the Red Lion. The two men standing to the fore on the right in the old photograph are Albert Ebenezer Fox and Ebenezer Albert Fox, the famous poaching twins from Stevenage. Their name is commemorated in the residential development Twin Foxes, built in 1998, with statues erected at the entrance.

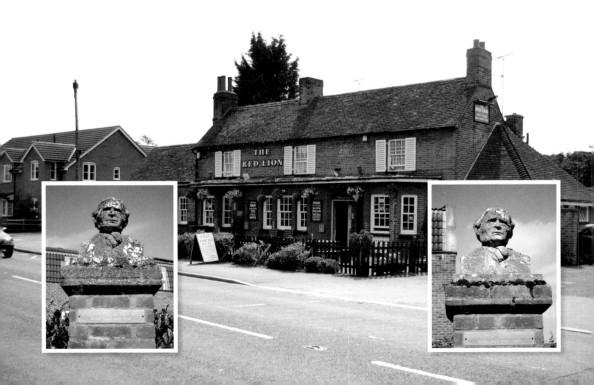

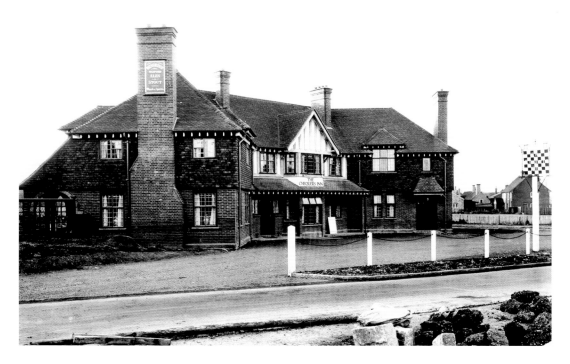

Woolmer Green Chequers

Both pubs on London Road in Woolmer Green belonged to the Hatfield brewery of Pryor Reid & Co. Some years after Pryor Reid was taken over by Benskins, the Chequers was rebuilt as a classic interwar 'road house', catering for the ever-increasing traffic on the A1. The earlier view shows the new building shortly after completion.

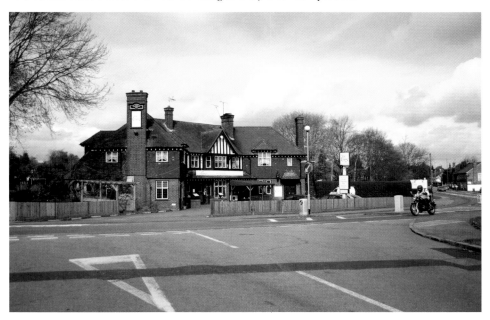

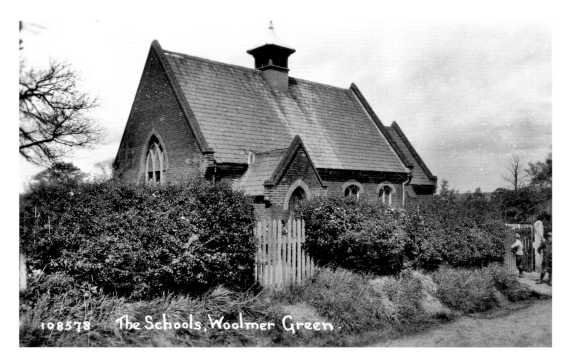

108578 The Schools, Woolmer Green.

Woolmer Green School

St Michael's primary school dates back to 1859 and has strong links with the church of St Michael and All the Angels across the road. Indeed, before the church was built in 1900, services were held in the school for twenty-two years. A new building, which today forms the main part of the school, was opened to the rear in 1971.

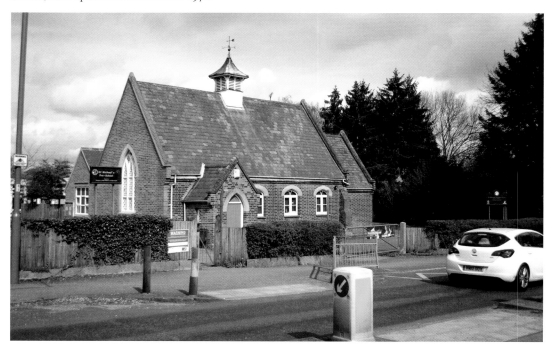

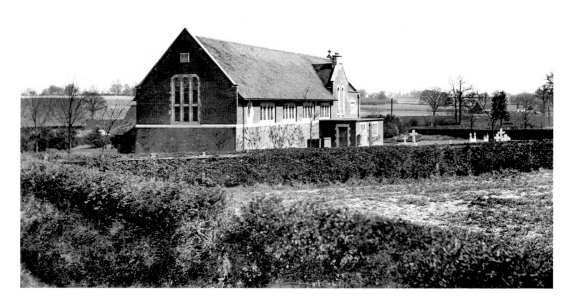

Woolmer Green Church

Woolmer Green obtained its own church in 1900, built in the Arts & Crafts style to the design of Robert Weir Schultz. Dedicated to St Michael and All Angels, the church stands on land donated by Lord Lytton.

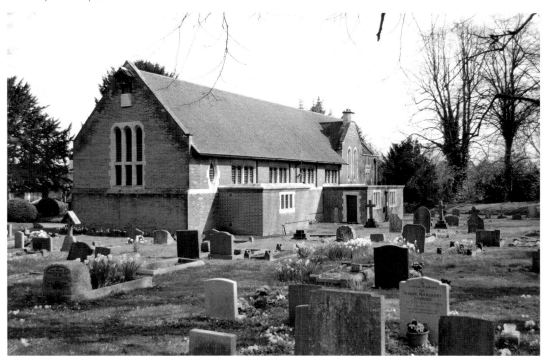

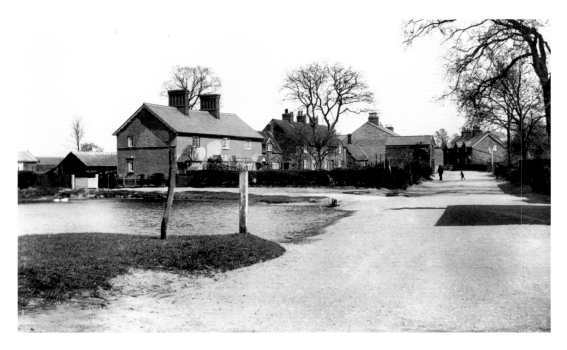

Woolmer Green Pond

Woolmer Green pond in New Road has been in existence since pre-Roman times. One explanation of the village's name is that it refers to the pond being 'the mere at which the wolves drunk'. Now the pond is no longer required to soak the wooden wheels of carts, a grass verge has been put between it and the road surface and, in 1975, it acquired a small island. In the distance on the right, the inn sign of New Road's pub, the Fox, can be seen. At one time this was the only tied house of Deards Welwyn brewery.

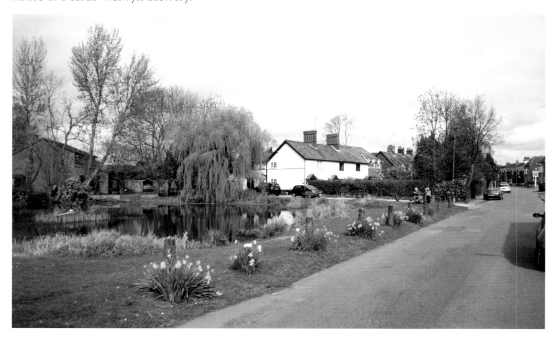

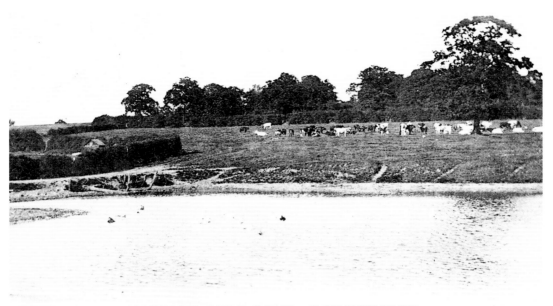

MARDLEY-BURY POND · DATCHWORTH

Woolmer Green, Mardleybury Pond

A large pond adjoins Mardleybury Road opposite Mardleybury Manor on the way to Datchworth. It is said to be haunted by the ghost of a young lady, who was thrown from a carriage that overturned on the bend in the road, drowning in the icy water. In 2011 it contained two large (and growing) catfish, one of 24lb and one of 36lb.

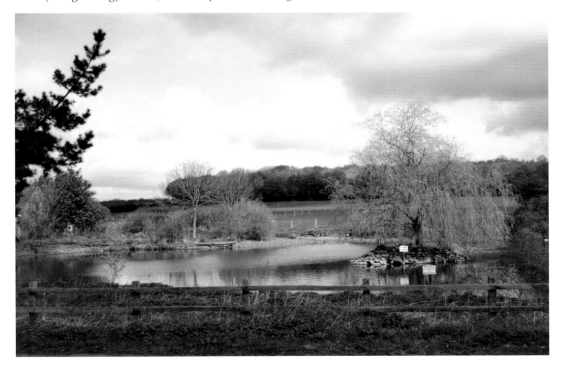

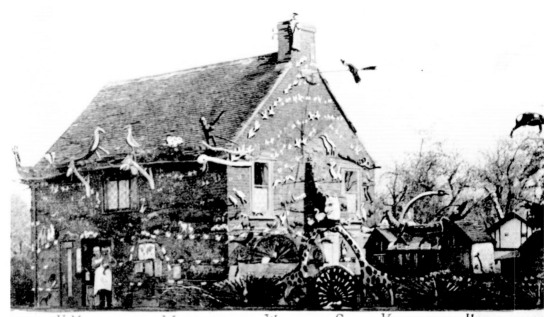

H. MACDONALD. WOODCARVER. WOOLMER GREEN. KNEBWORTH. HERTS.

Woolmer Green, Harry Macdonald's Carvings

The carpenter Harry Macdonald moved to Woolmer Green in 1937 and rapidly gained both local and national fame for his woodcarvings, which he formed into a vibrant display all over his house. Eventually, a model village was completed in his garden and thousands of visitors stopped by to enjoy his work. After his death in 1971 his carvings and house were destroyed and a new building was put up on the site. A blue plaque on a nearby house acknowledges his achievement.

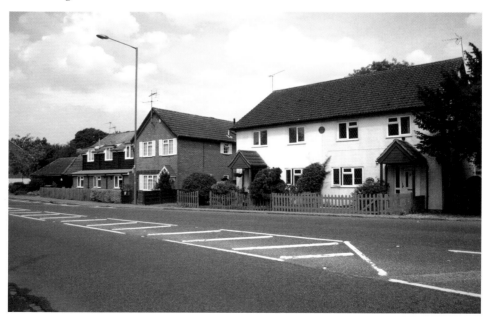